RUSSIA AND THE UNITED STATES

PITIRIM A. SOROKIN

has also written

LEAVES FROM A RUSSIAN DIARY

"Dr. Sorokin has produced a book which is likely to stand as one of the permanently valuable sources of information on Russian Revolution. But it is far more than a historical record. It is as vivid a narrative of human adventure under extraordinary conditions as Conrad or a Stevenson ever penned. With the utmost simplicity and modesty this remarkable man tells a story that makes the blood run cold."

—The Christian Advocate

THE CRISIS OF OUR AGE

"A book which stirs thought as few recent books have. THE CRISIS OF OUR AGE has already enjoyed a remarkable popular success for a book which can scarcely be described as popular, but it deserves to be far more widely read than it has been thus far." *—Professor* F. ASHLEY-MONTAGUE

MAN AND SOCIETY IN CALAMITY

"Here is a great scholar who is no Jeremiah. While admitting the great suffering which humanity in our time must endure from the four big evils which are the subject of his study, he does not despair. Calamities, he says, are not an unmixed evil; and, in a larger sense, have their compensation. . . . Dr. Sorokin has a profound truth to impart. . . . Lucid and thought-provoking and altogether stimulating."

The New York Times Book Review

Published by
E. P. DUTTON & COMPANY, INC.

RUSSIA
AND THE
UNITED STATES

PITIRIM A. SOROKIN

LITERARY CLASSICS, INC. DISTRIBUTED BY
E. P. DUTTON AND COMPANY, INC
NEW YORK   1 9 4 4

PRODUCING BOOKS IN WARTIME

THIS book has been produced in conformity with wartime economy standards.

The amount of reading matter has in no way been curtailed — there being more words per page.

Thinner books and smaller books will save paper, cloth, metals, transportation and storage space and will conserve manpower.

The publishers will do their utmost in meeting the objectives of the War Production Board towards the successful prosecution of the war.

S. A. JACOBS, THE GOLDEN EAGLE PRESS
MOUNT VERNON, N. Y.

CONTENTS

CONTENTS

PREFACE: *PRO DOMO SUA*

DURING the past few months I happened to give some public lectures on the topic of this book. After each lecture I was urged by members of the audience to publish these discourses because they found in them something new, enlightening, and valuable. Under existing conditions they considered that such a publication might serve the interests of both nations as well as that of a lasting peace. Being not unmindful of my social duties I decided to follow their suggestion. That is how this little volume happened to be written.

As to my qualifications for writing competently and without bias on the United States and Russia, a few words *pro domo sua* may not be amiss. Having been born in Russia and having lived there from 1889 to 1922, I naturally know Russia fairly well. I was born and reared within the lowest classes, subsequently passing through various strata of the Russian social pyramid from the status of a poor peasant and itinerant worker to the position of professor of law and sociology in the University of St. Petersburg and other institutions of higher learning, of a member of Kerenski's cabinet, of editor in chief of a metropolitan newspaper, of founder and member of the All-Russian Peasant Soviet, of member of the Council of the Russian Republic and the Constitutional Assembly, and so on. I thus lived the life of a poor peasant boy, itinerant artisan, factory hand, imprisoned revolutionary and counterrevolutionary, professor, journalist, political leader, and the like. Hence, to say nothing of my studies of Russia as a scholar, I may not unreasonably claim to know the Russian people and way of life, in their multifarious forms, fairly intimately.

Having lived in the United States from 1923 to the present time and discharged the duties of a sociologist, I believe that I have acquired also the requisite knowledge of this country. Being placed so fortunately in respect to both countries, I feel that I am in a position to compare their institutions fully as well as — perhaps even a little better than — those who know only one side of the topic.

As to possible biases in the delineation and interpretation of Russia, I was fortunate in enjoying an unusually objective orientation. Having been born and reared in the lowest and poorest Russian class, I can hardly be accused of bias in favor of the aristocracy and upper strata of society. Conversely, having studied the history of these classes and experienced direct and continuous contact with their best and worst representatives in a later period of my life, I am likely to be largely immune from the influence of the one-sided and distorted picture of the upper and middle classes created by the political propaganda of their violent opponents. The same is true of the Czarist and Communist regimes. Having fought the old regime and been three times imprisoned by it, I can scarcely be suspected of undue partiality toward it. Conversely, having been twice imprisoned by the Communist regime, condemned to death, persistently hunted from pillar to post as (in Lenin's words) "the most implacable leader of the Russian anti-Communist intelligentsia," and finally banished, I can hardly be biased in favor of the Communist system.

All in all, I would seem to occupy a relatively balanced position vis-à-vis both regimes, the various punitive measures applied to me tending to cancel out any bias I might otherwise entertain in regard to either.

Finally, my father being of Great Russian stock and my mother of Ugro-Finnish (Zyrian) stock, I am one of those ethnic "mongrels" who, in the opinion of Hitler, are among "the scum of the earth." This hybrid character has, however, its compensation; for as an ethnic mongrel I am naturally predisposed to view with the minimum of bias the problem of Russian nationalities.

Since this book is written for Americans, I have given much greater attention to Russia than to the United States; for while they know relatively little of Russia, they are well acquainted with their own country. If I were writing for Russians, the bulk of the space would, of course, be allotted to the United States.

Finally, a word about the leading principle of my interpretation and diagnosis. They are based not upon a calculation of motives, wishes, and fancies of this or that person in power, be it even a dictator or king or president. Deep and basic historical processes depend little upon an individual, no matter what is his position. They are determined by huge, collective, anonymous forces of the historical past of the nation, and by those of other nations, by a biological make-up of its population, and, finally, by its geographical milieu. My conclusions are based exactly upon a study of the constellation of these forces in both countries. Such a procedure appears to be much more valid than a guess-work of what this or that ruler is likely to do. If a ruler is going to stay in power he will exactly do what these huge forces will dictate. If he does not obey their dicta he is ousted from his power position. *Volentem fata ducunt nolentem trahunt.*

If this little volume serves even in a small way the purpose of engendering a better mutual understanding of the two great nations, I shall feel that my efforts have been amply rewarded.

I am indebted to Harvard Committee for Research in the Social Sciences for a financial help in typing and typographical preparation of the manuscript; to American Historical Association and to the Commission to Study the Bases of a Just and Durable Peace for a permission to reprint a part of my papers published in their publications.

PITIRIM A. SOROKIN

Harvard University

RUSSIA AND THE UNITED STATES

CHAPTER ONE

THE SIGNIFICANT LESSON OF
RUSSIAN-AMERICAN RELATIONSHIPS

1. *Enthusiasm and Apprehensions*

Our attitude toward Russia presents a peculiar contradiction. We are highly enthusiastic about the Russian Army: we praise its ability, its heroism and courage, its sacrifices; we feel very grateful to it for saving us and all the United Nations from utter catastrophe. At the same time many of us entertain serious suspicions and vague apprehensions respecting Russian Communism, atheism, "imperialism," and "barbarism." Some go so far as to find fault with Russia for *whatever* she does. If her armies retreat under the pressure of the German hordes, such detractors condemn her for her inability to defeat singlehanded the common enemy. They triumphantly shout: "Did we not tell you that the Red Army was good for nothing and would be cut to pieces in three weeks? Did we not warn against any entanglement with those impotent barbarians?" On the other hand, when the Red Army forces the German legions to retreat, such critics warn us gravely about the danger of a Muscovite invasion of Europe — the dire menace to civilization which would result from the victory of these twentieth-century "Scythians"! Their fundamental purpose is to see Russia's population and culture utterly exterminated and the earth freed from "such scum." Herein they are in complete accord with Hitler, Goebbels, and Company!

Others, while not going so far as these "saviors of civilization," nevertheless show the same trend. Take, for instance, the majority of the proponents of various types of "union now" and postwar alliances. Most such plans ignore both the desirability and the possibility of an intimate alliance with the Soviet Union, though they envisage a multitude of schemes for closer co-operation with Great Britain, France, Spain, Latin America, and even Germany. If an alliance with Russia is even mentioned in this connection, it is hedged about with all manner of safeguards designed to reduce her role in world affairs to the barest minimum.

2. *Momentous Questions and Answers*

Although the more extreme form of anti-Russian sentiment is not widespread, being confined largely to certain influential factions in this country and others of the United Nations of the West, the milder (contradictory) attitude of mingled enthusiasm and apprehension is entertained by a substantial percentage of the people of the United States and other countries. The prevalence of this attitude naturally raises the questions: To what extent is it justified? Does it have any valid basis? Is it to be seriously reckoned with in constructive planning for the postwar order? Should this country in particular strive for a close alliance with Russia, or should it avoid such intimate co-operation in its own interest as well as for the sake of the well-being of mankind?

These questions are highly important and must be clearly answered. *Throughout the entire history of the United States, Russia has been its best friend. If the respective governments do not commit the stupidest blunders, Russia will constitute in the future our best and most important ally. In the interest of both nations and of humanity at large, the most wholehearted co-operation is not only possible and desirable but essential. The chances for such co-operation between Russia and the United States are better, and those of an armed conflict are slighter, than the respective chances in the relations of either of these countries and any other great power. With-*

out the co-operation of these two nations no lasting peace is possible. If a new and nobler social order is to emerge from this tragic war, the United States and Russia must play a leading role in the work of reconstruction; and Russia will discharge its mission faithfully and wholeheartedly. If such an effort fails through insidious double-crossing on the part of egoistic nations, neither America nor Russia will be responsible for its miscarriage.

Such is my answer to the problem. It is clear. It differs markedly from many a current conjecture offered by so-called "experts" in international relations and socio-political planning. The subsequent pages of this book will demonstrate briefly the reasons for such an answer, and will indicate why my answer is more valid than most contemporary plans for postwar unions and alliances.

3. *The Miracle of Lasting, Unbroken Peace Between the United States and Russia*

The most decisive reason is *the unique and undeniable fact of an uninterrupted peace between these countries, extending throughout the entire history of the United States.* The utopia of a lasting peace between great powers has actually been realized in these relationships. Russia is practically the only major power with which the United States has never waged war, or even engaged in a single serious diplomatic conflict. A few minor diplomatic squabbles have, to be sure, occurred; but such petty clashes frequently mar the relations of even the various regions, provinces, or states of the same country. Moreover, the relations between Russia and the United States have been, for the most part, exceedingly warm, friendly, and co-operative. Throughout the greater part of the nineteenth century Russia was hailed in this country as "the best friend of the United States," and the United States was exceedingly popular in Russia. Let us note a few landmarks of this significant phenomenon.

France and Russia were the first foreign powers to help the United States as a sovereign nation. Already in 1779-1780 Russia was aiding this country in its struggle for independence through the armed neutrality of the League of Baltic Kingdoms organized by Russia and directed against England. As early as 1781 the United States was represented by Francis Dana at the Russian seat of government. Thereafter mutually beneficial diplomatic and social relations rapidly multiplied. In 1798 Russia offered the United States a coalition against France. In 1801 a close friendship, marked by frequent personal correspondence, was established between Czar Alexander I and Jefferson, each being a sincere admirer of the other. In 1807 the cordial relationship grew still warmer and more intimate. In 1812 Czar Alexander I offered to mediate between the United States and Great Britain. A number of agreements were concluded in 1812 and subsequent years concerning the neutrality and freedom of the seas and other important matters in which the interests of the two countries were identical. During this and subsequent periods Russia vitally assisted the United States to secure complete freedom of the seas for neutrals — a factor so important for the economic and political interests of this country. Russia and its "Prince of Peace," Czar Alexander I, were exceptionally popular among Americans at that time.

Later on, several other treaties were concluded to the mutual benefit of both nations. When one of the two countries happened to be in a difficult position, the other country usually came to its assistance. Thus, when Russia was attacked by a coalition of European powers in the Crimean War, the United States not only refrained from joining them but manifested its sympathy for Russia. Again, to cite a recent example, during the grave famine of 1921-1922 the American Relief Administration came to the rescue and saved, through its generous help, the lives of several millions of Russians. Similarly, when certain European powers threatened to intervene in American affairs during the Civil War, Russia sent her fleet with sealed orders to prevent such intervention. In this and other ways Russia vitally helped the United States during this difficult period. When, on top of this, Russia in 1867 sold Alaska to the United States for a mere $7,000,000, her popularity in the United States knew no bounds.

Only rarely — as at the end of the nineteenth century and again during the disastrous period of the Russian revolution of 1917 and the following years — has this unique friendship been clouded and the two countries shown a tendency to drift apart. But this temporary alienation never led either to war or to any serious diplomatic conflict. Even the sending of the American expeditionary forces in 1918 does not belie this statement: it was dispatched not *against* Russia but rather to *help* Russia. It was sent in response to explicit invitation on the part of various anti-Communist governments and sections of the population of Russia at a time when Germany still menaced Russia, and when the Communist government was as yet far from being firmly established. In addition, it was an insignificant force, and its military operations hardly amounted to anything that could properly be called war. Hence its activities in no way constituted an act of aggression against Russia.

Incidentally, it may be added that when both countries have happened to be involved in the same war, they have invariably been ranged on the same side, fighting a common enemy, whether in the case of the Boxer uprising, the war of 1914-1918, or the present war.

4. *The Significance of the Miracle*

The story of this remarkable relationship is highly significant and merits our attention for a number of reasons. In the first place, there are few cases in human history where two great powers, *in contact and interacting with each other,* have enjoyed unbroken peace for a period of 165 to 335 years (if we begin with the establishment of the English colonies on this continent). I know, to be sure, of several instances of prolonged peace between nations *isolated* from one another, without uninterrupted diplomatic and social relations. But I hardly know, in the entire range of Western history, another case of such protracted peace between great powers in *continuous interaction.*

It means that the age-old prayer of humanity "Glory to God in the highest, and on earth peace, good will to men," was actually answered in the case of the mutual relations of the United States and Russia. The phenomenon shines as a glorious solitary beacon in the dark and bloody history of the international conflicts of powers, proving that permanent peace between nations *is* possible. In this sense a token of hope, a source of unquenchable inspiration for a humanity aspiring for peace. Such is its first significance.

Its second lesson concerns all those who, at the present time, are preoccupied with plans for future social reconstruction. If they do not wish to build their temple of peace upon precarious foundations of wishful thinking, they must study carefully the real causes of the Russo-American miracle. If they can discover what these causes are, they can better understand the forces that work for peace and those that produce war. Without such knowledge only utopias doomed to failure can result. We shall presently see that most such projects are indeed destined to become complete fiascoes because they do not eliminate the causes of war or create the conditions necessary for a durable peace.

The third lesson applies to the "practical politicians," pseudo-patriots, and cynical "crusaders" who on every possible occasion either shout or whisper their contempt, suspicions, apprehensions, and forebodings concerning Russia — Russian "double-crossing," Russian Communism, Russian "militarism," and so on. For various reasons they find an alliance with the Soviet Union "dangerous," "undesirable," "impractical," or "unimportant." The unique record of unbroken peace with Russia is either forgotten or ignored. If their obsession were a mere personal hobby, it could be disregarded, for everyone is entitled to his own particular mania, provided it is *socially harmless*. In this case, however, the obsession may prove harmful for both countries, as well as for the rest of the world. To be sure, it can hardly wreck the long-standing harmonious cooperation of the two countries, which is based upon too powerful impersonal forces to be destroyed. However, under specific conditions the obsession in question might gravely prejudice the creative alliance.

We are now prepared to analyze the matter more deeply and to discover the underlying causes. A clarification of this issue not only may serve to prolong the peaceful relations existing between two great nations, but may be instrumental in extending the blessings of lasting peace to the international relations of other countries.

5. *The Main Cause*

How and why has unbroken peace been possible for such a long time between the United States and Russia? *It has been due mainly to the lack of any serious clash between the vital interests or basic values of the two countries, and it has been facilitated by the mutual mental, cultural, and social congeniality of the two nations.* In a subsequent chapter it will be shown that the principal and necessary cause of war has always been an irreconcilable conflict between the vital interests or the fundamental values of the societies involved. When and where such a clash occurs war ensues. In its absence, war either does not occur or else occurs infrequently and on a small scale. In the same chapter it is demonstrated that a similarity in mentality, social institutions, and culture is one of the most important supplementary forces working in favor of peace. (See also Chapters two and ten.)

No long or pedantic analysis is needed in order to see that the vital interests of Russia and the United States have never seriously conflicted, whether in the economic, political, territorial, or socio-cultural sphere. Both countries comprising vast continents, separated from each other by an ocean, neither of them was interested in *territorial encroachment at the expense of the other*. Each possessed sufficient territory, and each, in the process of expansion, naturally turned its attention to more accessible and more profitable areas than those of its distant neighbor across the Pacific.

The general situation is strikingly exemplified by such facts as the voluntary ceding of Alaska by Russia at the purely nominal price of some $7,000,000. We have no basis for claiming that Russia was forced to cede it under the military pressure of the United States, which was at that time (partly owing to the Civil War) militarily rather weak and a small power in comparison with Russia. No overt or hidden military pressure was exerted by the United States in this connection. Nor are we warranted in assuming that the Russian Government was simply stupid — unaware as to the great economic and strategic importance of Alaska. Anyone who has studied the history of the expeditions organized by the Russian Government throughout the seventeenth and eighteenth centuries and at the beginning of the nineteenth century for the exploration and annexation of Far Eastern Siberia, Kamchatka, the Kurile and Aleutian Islands, Sakhalin, the Bering Peninsula, and Alaska has ample evidence of its farsighted understanding of the enormous value and importance of these regions. Already in 1819 the net annual income of the nineteen Russian colonies on the American coast reached six million rubles. If, nevertheless, Russia sold Alaska, the reasons were sound and perfectly comprehensible: geo-politically,

economically, and militarily Alaska gravitated not to Russia
but to the United States (after this country had reached the
Pacific). A less friendly, territorially small power (hungry for
Lebensräum) would have pursued a different policy: such a
power would have tried to hold Alaska by all means, up to
armed conflict, since its retention would have constituted for
such a society a vital interest. For Russia — with its vast territory, and having at its disposal many regions more accessible, more easily developed, not separated by the enormous
distances of Siberia from the main centers of the Russian Empire, not divided by an ocean from the Russian mainland, and
not containing the germs of future military and other com-
plications — the cession of Alaska was in no way prejudicial
to any vital interest or basic value. Therefore Russia voluntarily sold it at practically a gift price.

Similarly, the purely *economic* interests of the two countries
have been free from any serious clashes. If anything, their
economic interests have been complementary, especially
after the development of industry in the United States during
a period when Russia was still only slightly industrialized.
There was no need for cutthroat competition for foreign
markets. Each country supplied its own chief market; each
possessed a vast territory of its own to develop; each could be
self-sufficient if the need for autarchy should arise. Moreover,
their geographic situation clearly defined the areas of their
primary economic influence: in such areas the other country
could not compete successfully even if it wished to do so.

On the other hand, as their international and diplomatic
history clearly shows, both countries had many common economic interests in respect to which they harmoniously co-
operated. Whether it was the principle of the "freedom of the
seas," or other economic interests defined in their diplomatic
agreements and treaties, both nations almost invariably found
their interests mutually advantageous. Hence their diplomatic
undertakings, as well as their reciprocal economic policies,

have been, as a rule, those of true allies. Being earlier industrialized than Russia, the United States directly and indirectly found in Russia a market for the products of its
industry — scarcely ever a competitor. Conversely, Russia
profited greatly by the economic, industrial, and technological experience of the United States.

The technological and industrial impact of America upon
Russia was already notable by the second half of the nineteenth century and has exerted an increasing influence up to
the most recent years: everyone knows the role played by our
technology and industry in the re-industrialization of Russia
during the period from 1921 to 1943. If Russia needed industrial products and economic guidance, it was only natural to
seek such assistance from the most highly industrialized and
technologically most advanced nation in the world — namely,
the United States.

In brief, the economic relations of the two countries have
proved in the main harmonious, complementary, and mutually beneficial. A certain amount of friction respecting secondary and relatively unimportant economic interests has, of
course, been inevitable, such as the disagreement concerning concessions for railroad building in China (by J. P. Mor-
gan; Kuhn, Loeb, and Company; and E. H. Harriman). But
such disagreements did not lead to war or even to any serious
diplomatic conflict. This essential harmony of interest promises further co-operation, although selfish, ignorant, and shortsighted groups may attempt to create a mountain of economic
conflict out of a molehill of petty antagonisms.

A similar absence of friction has prevailed in the *military*
field. Neither country has demanded, for the sake of strategic
security, any part of the territory of the other or any portion
of the territory of countries contiguous to the other. The only
possible area of conflict — Alaska — was, as we have seen, voluntarily ceded by Russia to the United States. From the military standpoint Russia has never manifested any interest in

American continental territory or in the islands on the eastern and western sides of the American mainland, with the exception of such islands as Sakhalin, adjacent to Russian shores. Nor has the United States been eager to acquire any part of the territory of Russia or of her sphere of military influence. The objective geographical status of the possessions of Russia and America has precluded any grave conflict in this field.

Conversely, the vital interests of the two countries have been closely intertwined through the exigencies of having to face common enemies. The case of Japan furnishes a notable example. That the policies of Japan and Russia have conflicted in the past and still do, and that they have led to war and may do so in future, is an obvious fact. The deep-seated antagonism began in the nineteenth century, became overt with the war of 1904-1905, and has continued up to the present time in the form of strained diplomatic relationships punctuated now and then by acute diplomatic conflicts and undeclared wars. This struggle is destined to continue. Until recently — even up to the attack on Pearl Harbor — many naïve Americans were blind to the irreconcilable clash of vital interests on the part of the United States and Japan and the inevitability of war between the two countries. These presumed "experts" stupidly believed and declared that *Russia, not Japan,* was the potential enemy of the United States — that Japan and America were destined to be *allies,* with mutually compatible interests. This explains in a large measure our pro-Japanese sympathies during the Russo-Japanese War of 1904-1905 and throughout the series of Nipponese aggressions between 1931 and 1939, as well as the fatuous policy of appeasement pursued up to the very day of the dastardly attack on Pearl Harbor. Meanwhile any competent — or even sensible — person familiar with the plans of Nipponese expansion blueprinted at least twenty to thirty years before the assault on Pearl Harbor knew full well that the interests of Japan dictated its main expansion not in the direction of

Siberia but toward the islands and continental territories to the southeast, south, and southwest of China — namely, Indo-China, Malaya, the Dutch East Indies, Australia, the Solomon archipelago, the Philippines, etc. — in a word, in *precisely* the direction in which Japan has moved since 1939. All this and many other perfectly obvious facts and symptoms, not to mention the relative geographic positions of the two countries, were ignored or grossly misconstrued by the "experts" in question. It required the actual outbreak of war in December, 1941, to convince them of the irreconcilable clash of vital interests in the relations of Japan and the United States and of the certainty of the continuation of the conflict in the future.

To sum up. In the present crisis, as well as on a number of occasions in the past, not only have the military interests of Russia and America failed to conflict but they have actually *merged* in the face of a common enemy. This explains why, when the two nations have participated in the same war, they have invariably been comrades in arms. This situation is destined to remain fundamentally unchanged for a considerable time to come. Only a deranged imagination can perceive in Russia a possible military danger. Only through the stupidest blunders of politicians and various "pressure groups" can a state of tension arise sufficiently acute to lead to war. The basic strategic solidarity of the two countries warrants the following conclusion: *the United States is less likely to become involved in war with Russia than with any other great power; and, conversely, Russia is less likely to become engaged in armed conflict with the United States than with any of the other first-class powers.* The same community of interest has marked, and will continue for an indefinite period to mark, their relations in the political, economic, social, and cultural spheres. Since an irreconcilable clash of vital interests constitutes the principal and necessary cause of war, the absence of such friction is sufficient to account for the amicable relations typical of the entire history of Russo-American contacts.

CHAPTER TWO

FACILITATING FACTORS: SOCIOCULTURAL SIMILARITIES

1. *The Role of Sociocultural Similarities in War and Peace*

"But," it may be objected, "how about the cultural values and social institutions of the two countries? What about the mentality and psychology of their peoples? Are not these as different as possible? Are they not mutually antagonistic, and has not this antagonism existed since long before the Russian Revolution? What common denominator can be found between prerevolutionary Czarist autocracy and American democracy; between the Communist dictatorship and the American republican regime; between militant atheism and free religion; between the illiterate prerevolutionary Russian peasantry and the relatively enlightened masses of America; between the mystical Russian *âme slave* and the realistic and pragmatic American mind; between the extreme emotionalism and sadness of the Russian soul and the balanced optimism of American psychology? From the psychological, cultural, and social standpoints Russia and the United States are at opposite poles. In so far as sociocultural and psychological interests or values are also vital values, they have certainly clashed. Therefore either your analysis of the causes of the aforesaid unbroken peace between the two countries is unsound or else sociocultural values, in your opinion, are not the vital interests — a thesis which is hardly acceptable."

At first glance the objection seems at once weighty and convincing. Yes, psychologically and socioculturally the two countries do differ in many ways. But so, too, in many respects, do the manners and mores, standards of living, tastes, education, religion, and psychology of various groups inhabiting the same city or two counties of the same state. However, these differences do not lead to civil war. The point is that we must distinguish between a mere disparity in the mental, cultural, and social values of two groups and an *irreconcilable antagonism* between these values. In this country the citizens belong to various occupations, political parties, religious denominations, nationalities, and clubs and associations; show different I. Q.'s; have different educational qualifications; and reveal different manners and ways of living. Yet these differences do not lead to armed conflict. The reason is that they are reconcilable — can exist side by side without any serious collision. Likewise two nations may disclose many psychological and sociocultural differences perfectly compatible with one another. Even if the American and Russian systems of psychological and sociocultural values were utterly diverse, this would not necessarily render them irreconcilable and therefore lead to war.

In the second place, the assumed fundamental discrepancy between the mental, cultural, and social values of the two nations has been greatly exaggerated. *As a matter of fact, the United States and Russia exhibit an essential similarity or congeniality in a number of important psychological, cultural, and social values.* These similarities fully counterbalance the differences. Hence they have functioned as facilitating factors in the record of undisturbed peace between the countries in question.

Mere social, cultural, and psychological kinship is not sufficient to insure peace between two countries, as is evident in the history of American and British relations. For this reason many a current plan for permanent peace is doomed to failure because the proposed "union" or "alliance" is based on a mere psychosocial and cultural affinity. Nevertheless, *in the absence of a clash between the vital interests of two countries, such an affinity does tend to promote peace, as in the case of Russia and America.*

Let us consider a few of the traits which they possess in common. Such an analysis will show the utter one-sidedness of the prevalent opinion, disclosing various significant characteristics of Russian society, culture, and psychology unfamiliar to foreigners.

2. Both Countries Are Vast Continents

Geo-politically, psychologically, and socioculturally this factor is highly important. Both countries are virtually continents in themselves. Both have vast deposits of mineral wealth that tend to make them self-sufficient. Both possess the widest variety of flora and fauna, climatic and geographic conditions ranging from the arctic to the semitropical, from those of high mountains to those of the prairie and plains regions. In so far as the totality of geographic, climatic, and geo-political conditions influences the mentality, culture, and social organizations of the inhabitants, the continental character of the two countries makes for essential similarity. It imposes upon both — for good or bad — *the role of a great power.* This role, in turn, brings with it dozens of economic, political, mental, and sociocultural functions inherent in the nature of a great power. Nationally and internationally it is bound to differ fundamentally from that of a small state. No important international change can take place without the participation of such a power. No "eternal neutrality" (like that of certain small states) can be assumed. It must surround itself with "satellite states" and "spheres of influence" to ensure its safety and must be separated by "buffer states" from other great powers. It cannot help being "imperialistic" (in a good or bad sense of the term). Unless it is protected by broad oceans (as was the United States until recently), it must possess a strong government, an army of officials and bureaucrats, a powerful military force, the cult of "a great empire," and the like.

Psychologically, this continental character favors broad mental horizons, vast perspectives, freedom from a narrow and meticulously calculated mentality, from the parsimonious policy in the economic, political, and sociocultural fields so common in the case of the small powers.

Socially and culturally this trait makes far-flung enterprises impossible, because of the lack of requisite resources, for the smaller nations — namely, huge economic corporations and other organizations, political adventures, efforts to create the foremost cultural centers, and so forth. When a nation is a great power, it seeks pre-eminence in literature and the drama, music and the fine arts, philosophy and religion, jurisprudence, economics, science and technology, etc. It aspires to possess the largest and most magnificent cities, the most brilliant court and society, the best universities, the finest cathedrals and museums, and the like. If its greatness lies only in territorial and military pre-eminence, and, moreover, is of brief duration, it sometimes fails to achieve these objectives. In most instances, however, they are realized in at least a few fields of cultural creativeness, as in the case of Egypt during the twelfth, eighteenth, and nineteenth dynasties; Assyria at the height of its power; China under the T'ang and other outstanding dynasties; the empires of the Guptas and Maurya in India; the powerful empires of Arabia; and those of Pericles, Alexander, Augustus, Queen Elizabeth and Queen Anne, Louis XIV, Peter the Great and Catherine the Great, and the United States (since the close of the nineteenth century).

In these respects, as has been pointed out, the role of the major continental powers is bound to contrast sharply with that played by the small powers, which simply do not have at their disposal the requisite natural and economic resources, sufficient man power, or adequate creative genius. They cannot afford to be reckless; must carefully budget, as it were, their mental, cultural, and social expenditures; must pursue a cautious, restrained, calculating, if not parsimonious, "bour-

geois" policy disdained by vast continental powers such as
Russia and the United States.

3. *The Relatively Peaceful Expansion of the Two Countries*

The next significant similarity is the comparatively peaceful
expansion of both countries to their continental dimensions.
In contrast to many past and present empires, *the expansion
has been achieved in both cases not so much by means of
military force as through the voluntary submission of various
tribes and peoples and through the peaceful penetration of
pioneers — mainly peasants or farmers, explorers, merchants,
and missionaries.* The creation of both empires has been
relatively peaceful — comparatively free from bloodshed, coercion, and cruelty. In the case of the United States this fact
is well known and needs no demonstration. In regard to
Russia it is far less well-known abroad. As a matter of fact,
the expansion of an insignificant state, that of Muscovy (embracing in the fourteenth century only about five hundred
square miles), into practically the vastest existing continental
empire in the world, and especially its expansion to the east,
to and beyond the Dnieper, to the Black Sea and the Caucasus,
and into Asia (beyond the line of the Volga) to Persia and
Afghanistan, China, and the Pacific — this growth has been
due primarily to the peaceful penetration of Russian peasants,
explorers, merchants, and missionaries, and partly to the
voluntary submission of numerous tribes and nationalities to
Russia. Only to a slight degree has it been achieved through
military conquest.

This expansion is a remarkable phenomenon from many
standpoints, and as such deserves a few additional comments.
It exhibits the Russian nation as a truly great empire-builder;
for it was accomplished not only contrary to all odds, by over-
coming superhuman difficulties, but with the minimum of

brutality, enslavement, or extermination in dealing with the subjugated groups.

It began under the relentless two-century-long Tatar domination of Muscovy and other Russian principalities. The struggle for liberation seemed to be hopeless. Yet it was unhesitatingly undertaken and carried on singlehanded, without the aid of any other Christian or non-Christian nation. The Christians, such as the Poles, Lithuanians, Livonians, and Swedes, and the Genoese and other European mercenaries, indeed did not hesitate to attack the Russian principalities, to despoil them, and at crucial moments actually to furnish military aid to their Tatar oppressors! Thus the army of the Tatar khan Mamai, who was seeking to crush Muscovy once for all as a punishment for its revolt, contained a number of "Western Christian mercenaries" who engaged the army of Dimitri Donskoi, the Grand Prince of Muskovy, in the battle of Kulikovo (1380). Moreover, the Christian nations had no scruples against buying up Russians prisoners, seized by the Tatars in their various incursions, and using them as *slaves*.

Nevertheless, the Tatar yoke was finally shaken off in 1480. The subsequent expansion westward consisted for the most part in a reconquest of ancient Russian principalities that had been seized by Poland, Lithuania, Livonia, Sweden, etc., achieved in a series of wars of liberation (and hence *essentially defensive* wars) which ultimately resulted in the reunion with Muscovy of most of the Russian states that had been annexed by western-European countries.

The expansion of Muscovy toward the south and east — especially up to and beyond the Volga, to the Caucasus, the Ural Mountains, Afghanistan, China, and the Pacific — exhibited a much more peaceful character. Muscovy regained the principality of Kiev, the most ancient Russian state, mainly through the voluntary submission of the population of this region and its hetman Bogdan Chmielnicki. In its hopeless struggle against persecution, plunder, and exploitation at the hands of the Poles and Turks, Kiev saw its only salvation in reunion with Muscovy. That the latter eventually reached the Caucasus was due largely to the voluntary subordination to Russia of the Christian Caucasian kingdom of Georgia. Wedged in between the then powerful Turkey and Persia, Georgia was wholly at the mercy of these non-Christian powers. As in the case of the Kiev region, its only salvation lay in becoming a Russian protectorate, a step which was taken by its king, Heraclius II, in 1783.

Another method of peaceful expansion consisted in the aforesaid steady penetration of peasants, explorers, merchants, and missionaries into regions either inhabited by primitive tribes or else totally uninhabited. This was the dominant mode of Russian expansion over Asia, from the Volga to Afghanistan, Manchuria, China, Bering Strait, and Alaska. These pioneers, like those of America, opened up, settled, and cultivated new regions largely without the assistance of the military forces of the State, though insignificant detachments of troops sometimes arrived after the initial occupation of the new lands.

The following examples may serve to illustrate this trend. A considerable part of Siberia — an enormous area lying between the Province of Perm (on the European side of the Ural Mountains) and the Rivers Irtysh and Tobol and the Chinese province of Sin-kiang — was acquired in 1587 by a private group of pioneers numbering only 840 men. The region of Siberia farther east, between Tobol and Lake Baikal, the River Lena, and Irkutsk, was similarly opened up by pioneers. Only after they had built blockhouses and established trading centers was a detachment of 130 men dispatched to the district (in 1641) to protect it against the attacks of certain tribes, the majority of the aborigines having voluntarily submitted to the Russian protectorate. The expansion of pioneers over the rest of Siberia, to the Sea of Okhotsk and the Pacific and Arctic Oceans, discloses an analogous record. The party that founded the Fort of Okhotsk consisted of but fifty-four men; the expedition that reached the Arctic, making a remarkable voyage from the mouth of the River Kolima around Bering Strait (in 1648), numbered only twenty-five men. Similarly, the parties that developed the valley of the Amur River, Manchuria, Kamchatka, the Kurile and Aleutian Islands, and Alaska, represented a mere handful.

The similarity to the expansion of the United States over the vast territory of America is obvious. To the credit of the pioneers of both countries it should be noted that they speedily converted the wilderness into centers of civilization, not only building blockhouses for self-protection but establishing trading centers, schools and churches, highways, a regular post service, and so forth, thus transforming hitherto desolate areas into well-populated agricultural and commercial regions. For instance, in 1662 the population of eastern Siberia amounted to scarcely 70,000, whereas by 1710 it had increased to 250,000.

What is still more remarkable is the fact that from the very outset these pioneers — and later on, the Russian State — treated the native population much more fairly and humanely than most other European colonizers treated the natives of subjugated colonies. The principal burden imposed upon the aborigines of Siberia was the payment of tribute in the form of furs. They were not exterminated, enslaved, or subjected to cruelty of any sort. Moreover, through conversion to Christianity they not only acquired an equal standing with Russians, civically and politically, but could enter the government service as officials and even intermarry with Russians. *There was never any racial discrimination.*

In order to expand — or even to survive — Russia was compelled to create a strong centralized government; and virtually all classes necessarily forfeited a good deal of their liberty in the process, having to render services that eventually amounted to practical serfdom. But these sacrifices of the strictly Russian population entailed *relatively few hardships for the indigenous population of the colonized areas.*

4. *Both Countries Exhibit Unity in Diversity*

Third essential similarity between the countries compared is the fact that *both are melting pots of diverse racial, ethnic, national, and cultural groups and peoples.* Russia, indeed, is a melting pot even more diverse than the United States. More than one hundred and fifty different ethnic groups, with different languages, peacefully coexist there side by side. This fact of *unity in diversity* exerts a powerful influence upon the psychology, culture, and social life of both countries. It makes their mentality broader and more receptive than that of peoples constituting a single ethnic group. It gives to that mentality and culture a greater variety, a greater richness, than that enjoyed by the mentality and culture of any one ethnic group, because each of the numerous nationalities and races makes its own peculiar contribution to the total culture of the nation. As we shall see later on, the United States and Russia, especially since the middle of the nineteenth century, have been progressively coming of age — possibly more successfully than most of the other European nations. One of the reasons has been precisely this diverse composition of their population from the racial, ethnic, and cultural standpoints.

This phenomenon has another important value. It presents a united nation whose unity is based not upon the ethnic or racial homogeneity of its population but upon its *diversity.* This is a kind of social body profoundly different from that composed of a single homogeneous group. Hitler and many others assure us that only such a homogeneous body, made up of one people, one nationality, one culture, one language group, can possess a real unity and real value. The case of the United States and of Russia is a direct repudiation of such claims. These two countries demonstrate clearly not only that unity in diversity is possible but that such a unity may be as strong, creative, and indestructible as that of any social body consisting of a single race or ethnic group. Hitler's experience during this war must convince him of his fallacy. He expected that under his powerful attacks the Russian and American melting pots would crack at once. In this expectation he adopted the policy of promoting the narrow egoism of various racial and ethnic groups in Russia and America by fostering their separatism, their mutual antagonisms, and their exclusive interests. The objective result was a complete fiasco: instead of a disintegrated Russia he was confronted with a nation united as never before, with all its ethnic groups fighting heroically against the invader. In a somewhat different form he experienced the same disillusionment in the case of the United States. In both cases the "cracking melting pot" turned out to be an indivisible, indestructible, unity as firm and strong as any society could possibly be.

This fact has a still further significance, not only for the present but also for the future. If a united nation were possible only when it is made up of but one race or ethnic group, all hopes for a future united mankind, for a world federation, for even unions of two or more separate nations, based upon genuine equality and freedom, would be doomed unconditionally. In this case, only a union of the "master race" with its enslaved subjects, bound by bloody coercion, would be possible. That is exactly the ideology and policy of the Hitlerites and their partisans. The United States and Russia demonstrate clearly the utter fallacy of such theories and practices. They prove that unity in diversity, based not upon the domination of a master group and the slavery of "inferior" groups but upon true equality is possible. In neither country is there any serious problem of national or racial minorities, of separatism, of ethnic or racial antagonisms. All elements live peacefully and proudly side by side, each on an equal footing, each given equal opportunity to unfold its creative forces, without any distinction of masters and slaves, of dominant and subordinate groups, of superior or inferior elements. To be sure, a few traces of inequality still remain, since the great social experiment is not yet concluded; but these are *only remnants*. In a word, both countries are huge laboratories successfully performing a notable social experiment — that of creating a united society out of diverse elements bound together by the bonds of equality and free solidarity. Moreover, this experiment shows that the unification of mankind — or of its greater part — is indeed possible and points to the surest method for the achievement of this great objective.

With regard to Russia it should be noted that this experiment was inaugurated not with the Russian Revolution but long before it. In a sense it dates from the emergence of the first Russian principality. Instead of beginning with a conquest, it starts with the voluntary summoning of Scandinavian chiefs to administer governmental, especially military, functions. In this way was established the first dynasty of Russia, that of the Scandinavian Rurik. Privileged positions were voluntarily given by the Russian tribes to a non-Russian nationality. Since that time the upper and ruling classes have been recruited from all races and ethnic groups, both domestic and foreign. The aristocracy and ruling class of the principality of Muscovy was a veritable melting pot. Its most aristocratic families were composed not only of Russian but also of non-Russian stocks: of the descendants of the Lithuanian dynasty the Gedymins, such as Golitzyn and Troubetzkoi; of outlaws from Germany, like Tolstoi and Scherbatov; of Finnish and Tatar stocks, represented by Mescherski, Mordvinov, and Ourousov; of those of Caucasian origin, as Tcherkassky; and so forth. Some of these non-Russian aristocrats even became Czars, like Boris Godunov. Especially noteworthy was the proportion of the upper classes consisting of non-Russian stock from the time of Peter the Great on. Peter spared no pains to attract talented foreigners to Russia, and, like his successors, lavished upon them the highest positions and honors. Under his successors Scots, French, Dutch, Jews, Italians, Georgians, Poles, Lithuanians, Tatars, Mongolians, and especially Germans, were represented in the upper classes in a ratio out of all proportion to their share in the total population of Russia.

During the period between Peter the Great and Alexander I the infiltration of Teutons became positively overwhelming. It eventually proved a worse source of oppression for the Russian population than even the Tatar domination. The Kurland-Brunswick-Holstein factions, consisting largely of stupid, greedy, cruel, Russian-hating elements, seized even the Russian throne itself. The czars and czarinas of that period (Catherine I, Anna Ioanovna, Peter III) had little or no Romanov blood, representing primarily or exclusively a third-class Teuton strain. All the leading positions in the army, the navy, and the government (including the dictatorial position of Biron, the most disgusting ruler Russia ever had), were pre-empted by these factions. "Russia, according to a contemporary chronicler, was converted into a trading mart for the spoils of thieves." The Birons, Münnichs, Ostermanns, Löwenfelds, etc., with their legions of Kurland, Brunswick, and Holstein followers, together with Jewish advisers like Lipmann, wrote one of the darkest chapters in the whole of Russian history.[1]

A recruitment of the ruling class from the most diverse nationalities has continued up to the present day. Scions of the Polish aristocracy, like the Radzivills and Chartoryjsckys; of the so-called Ukrainian aristocracy, like the Kotchubeys; persons of Georgian, Finnish, French, Scotch, Jewish, and espe-

---

[1] Generally speaking, the influence of the otherwise great German nation upon Russia has been rather negative. It never gave to Russia its Kants and Beethovens, its Goethes and Schillers, or even its Bismarcks and other creative minds. Instead, it supplied for the most part either mediocre or greedy or brutal elements. As a result the contribution of Russo-Germans to Russian culture — its literature, music, sculpture, painting, drama, science and philosophy, religion, law and ethics, political and military leadership — has been very modest. In brief, with a few exceptions Russia has derived from Germany mainly its scum.

cially German stocks — these have continued to fill its ranks
out of all proportion to their percentage of the total population. The same is true of the professional and other middle-
class elements. In other words, not only the population as a
whole but especially its upper and middle classes have constituted a veritable melting pot of Russian and non-Russian —
particularly Teutonic — stocks.[2] If any nationality has been
discriminated against in its representation within the upper
classes, it has certainly been the Great Russian, Little Russian,
and White Russian nationalities — that is, precisely those
which have been the chief creators of the Russian Empire and
Russian culture, and which even now, after the absorption
into the empire of some 150 to 175 different ethnic groups,
represent approximately 77 to 80 per cent of the total
population.

The perpetuation of this historic tradition is revealed by the
contemporary composition of the Soviet government. Its dictator is a Georgian, Stalin (Dzhugashvili); his right-hand man
is a Russian (Molotov); his next-closest associate is a Jew
(Kaganovich). Then come a host of other political bosses —
a veritable potpourri of the most diverse nationalities and
ethnic groups, in which the Russian nationality (80 per cent
of the total population) plays but a modest role.

Thus we see that Russia has always been a genuine melting
pot of various ethnic and racial groups; that they have all co-
operated in this unity in diversity, each contributing its share
to Russian culture and the Russian state; and, finally — contrary to a widely current but fallacious opinion — that this
unity was not based upon a compulsory privileged domination
of the Russian nationality over the others. It is true that the
Russian nationality has been the primary creator of the Rus-

[2] The following incident well illustrates the preponderance of German stock.
When Czar Nicholas I asked Ermolov, the conqueror, organizer, and admin-
istrator of the Caucasus, "What reward dost thou want for thy services?"
Ermolov ironically answered, "Your Majesty, make me a German!"

sian state and Russian culture. But it has borne the brunt of
the labor and sacrifices, including the work of fighting.[3] A
disproportionately large share of blood, sweat, toil, disfranchisement, and even serfdom has fallen to its lot, while it has
enjoyed a comparatively small share of the rewards and
privileges (see Chapter four, §5).

I reiterate. The alleged ruthless domination by the Russian
nationality over other ethnic groups is a *sheer myth*. I fully
realize that to many this statement may sound incredible. A
host of objections at once arise: "But how about the limitation,
for instance, of the rights of the Poles? of the Jews? of the
Finns? Is it not true that they were deprived of many rights
enjoyed by the Russian nationality?" The contention sounds
plausible enough and has been used to decry the alleged
persecution of the non-Russian elements. However, a closer
study of the Polish, the Finnish, or even the Jewish situation
in prerevolutionary Russia leads to a radically different
conclusion.

Let us begin with *Poland*. Several centuries of bitter struggle
between Poland and Russia formed the background for their
more recent relations, weighing heavily upon the last century
and a half of their mutual attitude. The unfortunate partition
of Poland was primarily not a Russian but a European affair,
although Russia participated in it and hence had to bear its
share of blame. The entire matter belongs to the field of international warfare. As such it is not a question of how the Poles
were treated as citizens of Russia. When we turn to this question, the decisive facts are as follows. In spite of bitter historical memories, and notwithstanding the fact that Poland had
fought on the side of Napoleon in his invasion of Russia, never-

[3] Even at the present time, if the representation of the Russian nationality in
the Soviet political aristocracy is disproportionately low, its share among the
fighting forces is rather disproportionately high; for the Red Army is over-
whelmingly Russian in nationality, and more than 90 per cent of its generals
(Shaposhnikov, Joukov, Vatutin, Voronov, Rokassovsky, Timoshenko, etc.)
and other officers are Russians.

theless, when Russia had defeated Napoleon, Czar Alexander I, in opposition to Metternich and other European diplomatists, achieved the creation of a new kingdom of Poland, granting to the Russian part of Poland a constitution, parliamentary self-government, and the right of possessing its own army — *privileges most of which were not enjoyed by the citizens of Russia proper.* In his letter of May, 1813, to the President of the Polish Senate, Count Ostrovsky, Alexander I wrote: "If the great interest of general peace has not permitted (owing to the opposition of Austria and Prussia P. S.) the union of all the Poles under the same scepter, I have tried at least to soften, as far as possible, the rigor of their separation, and to obtain for them everywhere the maximum enjoyment of their nationality." On June 21, at Warsaw, the new kingdom was solemnly inaugurated, with Alexander I as king of Poland, and endowed with the aforesaid liberal constitution and with privileges far greater than those enjoyed by the citizens of Russia proper. In spite of a wave of reaction throughout Europe, the Polish constitution and its parliamentary self-government (including unrestricted freedom of debate and decisions) were preserved for many years.

The radical departure from this generous and enlightened policy was due to the revolt of the Polish nobility in 1830 and especially in 1863. These rebellions were naturally regarded as the breach of a solemn contract on the part of Poland, whereby the Russian Government was freed from its obligation to maintain the constitution and other special privileges enjoyed by Poland. However, even this change operated essentially to the detriment of the nobility, proving rather beneficial to the peasantry, who had been ruthlessly exploited by the nobles. This policy led to the emancipation of the Polish serfs by the Russian Government, a measure which was carried out under conditions far more advantageous for the Poles than for the serfs of Russia proper. After their emancipation the latter had to pay their former masters a considerable sum of money for the land they received, whereas the Polish serfs were exempted from such compensation. Moreover, the Polish peasants were allowed to retain all the land that they held in copyhold, whereas those of Russia proper obtained only a part of such land.

After the rebellion of 1863, as a natural reaction to it, certain limitations of Polish rights were introduced, mainly concerning such matters as the acquisition and tenure of land, the holding of Catholic religious processions in public, and the compulsory study of Russian as the official language of the empire. Such restrictions, however, were in no way particularly harsh. If anything, they were milder than the treatment of similar rebellious groups by most other nations, such as the treatment of the Irish rebels by Great Britain, of the Southern rebels by the United States immediately after the Civil War, and of the Poles at the hands of Austria and Germany.

Toward the close of the nineteenth century and at the beginning of the twentieth most of these disabilities were abolished. In the twentieth century the Poles in Russia enjoyed approximately the same status as that of the rest of the Russian population. Not only in Poland but throughout the whole of Russia the Poles were on an equal footing with the Russians, occupying a prominent place in the government service, in all the professions, and in other high positions, and making a distinct contribution to Russian culture.[4]

The net conclusion of this brief survey is that if Russia did not treat the Poles with ideal generosity — especially after,

[4] For instance, during my student days at the University of St. Petersburg, there were numerous Polish professors. Some of them, such as my distinguished teacher Professor L. Petrajitzki (probably the most eminent legal theoretician of the twentieth century), the famous classicist T. Zelinsky, and the brilliant philologist Baudoin de Courtenay, occupied the very forefront of their profession, wrote all their works in Russian, and never complained of any unjust treatment. Curiously enough, on their return, after 1917, to their native land, they found their Polish compatriots uncongenial and that they as scholars were appreciated much less than they were by Russia.

having been granted a constitution and various other privileges, the Poles proved rebellious — nevertheless their treatment by Russia was on the whole fully as generous as that accorded such a conquered nationality under similar historical conditions by any other power, and certainly more liberal than the treatment of similar groups by many Western powers. Prior to the rebellions of 1830 and 1863 the Poles enjoyed far greater privileges than those bestowed upon the population of Russia proper; and ultimately they were accorded virtually the same status as that of the Russians themselves.[5]

Very similar — and still more generous — was *the treatment of Finland by Russia up to the beginning of the twentieth century*. Here again the prevalent notion abroad is completely erroneous. In the first place, Russia did not rob Finland of her independence; for Finland had never been a sovereign nation. Before passing to Russia after the Swedish-Russian War of 1808-1809, it had been subject to Sweden. The period of Finnish history under Sweden, by the way, was far from a happy one.

Second, when, as a result of the defeat of Sweden, Finland passed to Russia, the same Czar Alexander I who later granted a constitution to Poland gave to Finland a national existence which she had never possessed before. Finland was made a grand duchy and given a liberal constitution, with the Russian Czar as grand duke. She was granted practically complete self-government in all her internal affairs,[6] with a diet and various other privileges not enjoyed by the rest of Russia.

[5] I regret to add that after the reconstruction of Poland following the First World War the treatment by the Poles of their national minorities — the Great Russians, the White Russians, and the Ukrainians — was decidedly harsher and more oppressive than that of the Poles at the hands of Russia, even during the worst period of Russian "oppression." Judged by this standard, the lot of the Poles under the Russian regime was a highly fortunate one.

[6] It was so wide that Finland became a safe refuge for Russian revolutionists: as soon as they escaped into Finland they were safe from the Czarist government: it did not violate Finnish autonomy even in these matters. This explains why Finland became one of the centers of activities of Russian revolutionaries.

She was exempted from military duty, obligatory for the rest of the Russian population. In addition, railways, fortresses, universities, museums, and so on were constructed largely at the cost of the Russian empire. This period of wide internal autonomy, from 1809 to the beginning of the twentieth century, was certainly one of the brightest in the entire history of Finland. During the nineteenth century, under Russia, Finland enjoyed a real renaissance of her social, political, and cultural life.[7]

Third, it was only at the very close of the nineteenth and the beginning of the twentieth century, after the appointment of Bobrikov as the personal representative of the emperor, that certain measures were introduced that tended to limit somewhat the liberties and privileges of Finland. The main item in these "oppressive" measures was the insistence of the Russian Government that the Finns should render military service. Such a change of policy arose from altered conditions, including the growing incapacity of the decadent old regime in Russia. But even these restrictions left Finland in a position far more privileged than that of the rest of Russia.

Fourth, with the Revolution of 1917 the Kerenski regime abolished all these limitations and promised the complete sovereignty of Finland. This promise was realized within the next three years, and since that time Finland has been wholly independent of Russia. The civil war that followed this transfer of sovereignty was a struggle between the Communist and anti-Communist factions — not a war with Russia.

This brief outline of Russo-Finnish relations shows that Finland was treated rather more generously than the Russian population itself and was accorded a status to be envied by the rest of Russia.

Finally, a word about the aggression of Soviet Russia against

[7] All this and much more is stated by Finnish minister of foreign affairs, A. Hackzell, in his address in Berlin, 1939, published as "*Finnland's Stellung*" in *Ost-Europa*, March-April, 1939.

Finland in 1939. Formally it was an act of aggression, though actually it was something very different. Neither Stalin nor anyone else had any apprehension that Finland as such could be dangerous to Russia. But every competent person knew that, as a debtor nation, Finland had become a sort of ward of Great Britain, the United States, Germany, and Sweden. Between 1920 and 1939 she had borrowed such large sums of money that, at the very best, many decades would be required to pay off these debts. Thus she had become a borrower, of doubtful solvency, dependent upon the governments and capitalists of various countries.[8]

What is more important, with the rise to practically dictatorial power of the Mannerheim clique in Finland, she became a mere military appanage of Germany, which, after the accession of Hitler, began definitely to prepare Finland as a base for the invasion of Russia. This was no secret to Stalin and anyone else concerned in the matter. Finland as such was perfectly harmless to Russia. But Finland utilized by a great power in its plans for the invasion of Russia, with a boundary only twelve miles from Leningrad, was a real menace to some 180 million of Russians. No statesman responsible for the safety of his country could tolerate such a situation. When all peaceful means to adjust it failed, Russia was compelled to engage in a preventive war. Such was the real nature of this so-called aggression — a conclusion unequivocally corroborated by the subsequent alliance of Finland with Germany and by their joint invasion of Russia.

At present, Finland finds herself in the most tragic situation, thanks to its Mannerheim-Rity faction. On the other hand, one must not forget that in the siege of Leningrad alone (besieged by the German-Finnish forces) about 1,500,000 per-

[8] The "honesty" of Finland, so highly praised in the United States, in meeting the interest payments due on American loans, is a facile type of honesty consisting in repaying merely an insignificant fraction of the money which she had received from this country.

sons—that is, the equivalent of approximately half of the whole population of Finland — perished. From any truly humanitarian standpoint this result of the German-Finnish aggression amply compensates for all the "aggressions" of Russia against Finland. Another significant fact is the development of the imperialistic appetites of the Mannerheim-Rity regime after the initial successes of the German-Finnish invasion of Russia, as evinced by the seizure of parts of Russia that had never belonged to Finland, as well as by the serious discussion of a "Greater Finland" incorporating enormous Russian territories and even areas of Scandinavia that had never in any way been related to Finland.

Let us turn now to the thorny *Jewish* question. Here again the real situation is quite different from the one popularly assumed outside Russia. First, the persecution of the Jews is not a Russian monopoly but a world-wide phenomenon, in a sense universal and perennial, dating from ancient Egypt and Rome and extending up to the present time.

Second, prior to the sixteenth century Russia was less guilty of this sin than the Europe of the medieval and Renaissance periods. Up to this century there were no historically recorded persecutions of Russian Jews, whereas throughout practically the whole of Europe during the Middle Ages and even up to approximately the time of the French Revolution the Jews suffered severe persecutions and drastic limitations of their rights. This explains why they settled in such great numbers in Poland, Lithuania, and Russia during those centuries.

Third, Russia subsequently followed the example of Europe and introduced various restrictions, now decreasing (as under Alexander I and Alexander II), now increasing (as during the reigns of Nicholas I and Alexander III), which continued up to the beginning of the twentieth century, a few persisting even up to the Russian Revolution of 1917. The principal disfranchisement consisted in a limitation of the territory in which Jews could settle, several western provinces being set aside for this purpose. At the same time, all Jews with certain educational or technical training, engaged in certain occupations, or possessing capital were free to settle wherever they pleased. This explains why Jews could be found in every city of Russia. Such Jews enjoyed virtually all the rights accorded Russian citizens. Other restrictions, such as the percentage norm (4 per cent of the total number of students) established for Jews entering colleges and universities, and certain limitations of property rights in land (designed to prevent Russian peasants from falling into financial dependence upon Jews and from selling their land to Jews and to commercial urban dealers in general), were real disfranchisements, though by no means cruel or inhuman. Moreover, these limitations were actually much less onerous than they appear on the statute books. For instance, the 4 per cent norm limiting the number of Jews entering universities and colleges exceeded the proportion of the Jewish population in the total population of Russia (namely about 1.8 or 2 per cent). Moreover, the actual percentage of Jewish students was far larger even than 4 per cent. Likewise, the proportion of Jews within the commercial, professional, and governmental classes was considerably greater than their share in the total Russian population. Their contributions to Russian culture were far more decisive and fruitful than one can judge on the basis of formal legal provisions. The same is true of many other Jewish disabilities. Such discriminatory legislation, being unpopular with the Russian people as a whole, was to a large extent a dead letter.

Another mitigation of Russia's sin in this matter is found in the fact that the Jews were officially discriminated against not for racial or ethnic reasons but almost exclusively on *religious* grounds. Hence as soon as a Jew chose to become a Christian, he was freed from all restrictions and became a full-fledged citizen. This is one of the reasons why the Jews were able to play so notable a role in the highest official circles, even under such autocrats as Nicholas I. Thus his Minister of

Finance, Count Kankrin, was a Jew, and for some twenty years (at the end of the nineteenth and at the beginning of the twentieth century) an Armenian Jew named Delanov was Russian Minister of Education. These cases are in no way exceptional.

Again, it should be noted that Russia never pursued the diabolical, cold-blooded, calculated policy of systematic exploitation, humiliation, and downright extermination which has marked not only the Hitler persecutions but the oppression of Jews in many other countries of the past and present. As has been said, the Jews were never discriminated against as a racial or ethnic group. (Thus, intermarriage between Jews and Gentiles was not prohibited in Russia.) This explains the curious fact that the most effective propagandists of Russia abroad have always been former Russian Jews. While they have roundly denounced the Czarist regime (often with undue severity), they have entertained the warmest feelings toward Russia itself.

There remains the notorious matter of *pogroms*. Their actual number has been vastly exaggerated. So also has been the number of their victims, who have totaled far fewer than the total number of victims of lynching in the United States. Moreover, they occurred only at the turn of the present century and are chargeable solely to a small clique of governmental and semigovernmental gangsters. The overwhelming mass of the Russian population always emphatically disapproved of these crimes and were hence guiltless of them.

We may now return to the main thesis of this chapter — namely, to the consideration of Russia as a "unity in diversity," as a melting pot, as one of the few notable experiments in building a closely knit society out of diverse elements without any clear-cut division of these elements into superior and inferior, into master and slave, into privileged and disfranchised. The foregoing analysis proves that, if not in the ideal yet in a relative sense, Russia, like the United States, has realized these possibilities. The work of the Revolution in this field has been but a continuation and consummation of this perennial trend of Russian history. The last vestiges of discrimination — legal and otherwise — against the Jews and the other one hundred and fifty different nationalities have finally disappeared. Each enjoys an equal opportunity to develop its creative potentialities in terms of its own peculiar culture, language, and inclinations; and each is encouraged to do so. All of them have their own schools, and books published in their respective tongues. Although the Russian tongue, as the historical language of Russia and of its dominant nationality, is (like English in our country) the common medium of expression, this in no way militates against the free use of the one hundred and fifty other languages spoken throughout the Soviet Union.

Even such a detail as the official replacement of the name "Russia" by the term "Union of Soviet Socialist Republics" (suggestive of "the United States of America") is a logical development of the phenomenon in question, as is also the multi-national composition of the present Soviet ruling class. In this, as in many other respects, the Russia of the constructive phase of the Revolution represents a perpetuation (as we shall see later on) of the vital trends of prerevolutionary Russia.

CHAPTER THREE

AMERICAN AND RUSSIAN SOULS

1. *The Myth of the "Âme Slave"*

The next basic similarity between Russia and America lies in the psychology and mentality of the two nations. By this similarity is not meant, of course, either *identity* or *complete homogeneity* of mental, emotional, affective, and volitional characteristics. There are no two Russians or two Americans who are exactly identical. Both peoples exhibit thousands of mental types. The first point is that the notion of a peculiar *âme slave* (or Slavic soul) — vague and mystical, impractical, sad, highly emotional, unstable, oscillating between moods of ecstasy and profound depression — is an absurd fiction. The Russian soul is commonly supposed to be diametrically opposed to the alleged *âme américaine*, which is conceived of as being invariably sober, balanced, rational, practical, free from undue emotionalism, and completely unmystical. This notion is equally fantastic. In both countries these two types, and many other types, probably exist in approximately equal percentages. If any conspicuous difference is to be found in the distribution of such psychological types, it is to be explained principally in terms of different historical periods and their specific social circumstances — not as something perennial and inherent, rooted in the biological constitutions of the respective peoples.

No profound and perennial disparity in the psychology of the two nations can be ascribed to their *racial make-up; because racially, or anthropologically, the Russians do not differ fundamentally from the Americans.* The bulk of the Russian population belongs to the so-called Alpine and Nordic types. Apart from the Mongolian and Asiatic groups, comprising some 8 per cent of the Russian population, the average cephalic index is around 82, a considerable part of the population has an index below 82, and another portion has an index slightly above 82. From the standpoint of this important criterion the Russians do not differ appreciably from the bulk of the population of northern and central Europe, including Switzerland, Germany, Austria, France, and northern Italy. If anything, they are slightly more Nordic than the inhabitants of central Europe, including France. In addition, they are more homogeneous, showing some three points of variation from 82 in both directions, while the range of the cephalic index of France, Germany, and central Europe fluctuates more widely. From the standpoint of the color of eyes, and hair — another racial criterion — we find about 67 per cent of blondes among the Letto-Lithuanians, 57 per cent among the White Russians, 40 per cent among the Great Russians, and 35 per cent among the Ukrainians — all in all approximately 45 to 50 per cent for the European and non-Asiatic population of Russia. In comparison with France, Brandenburg and Prussia, Switzerland, southern Germany, Czechoslovakia, Italy, Spain, and many other countries, the majority of the Russians incline more in this respect to the Nordic or Alpine type. The same is true of stature and other racial criteria.

In so far as the population of the United States is composed primarily of European immigrants, it cannot be fundamentally different from the ethnic types of Europe or Russia. If Russia is ethnologically 8 to 10 per cent Asiatic, the United States exhibits an approximately similar proportion of Indians, Negroes and Asiatics. Otherwise, the chief difference in racial composition is that the United States possibly possesses a somewhat greater proportion of Mediterranean and extreme Nordic types. These factors are, however, too negligible to make any serious difference in the respective psychologies of the two peoples, even if we assume that specific mental types are connected with specific racial constitutions. As a matter of fact, all attempts to prove such a connection have thus far failed. Therefore their ethnological composition cannot afford a valid basis for assuming any inherent and perennial differences in their national psychology. And no other basis for such claims exists.

Hence if any typical differences in the mentality of Americans and Russians are found, they must be *acquired* traits, due to changing environmental or historical circumstances. As such they are neither perennial nor inherent but temporary and local, varying according to the sociocultural conditions. For instance, in view of the Revolution of 1917, many are prone to think that the Russians are naturally *revolutionary* in temperament, whereas the Americans, English, and Dutch are conservative and orderly peoples. But in the seventeenth and eighteenth centuries the English and Americans were more revolutionary than the Russians. If one surveys all the revolutions in the history of Russia, Poland, England, Holland, France, Germany, Spain, Italy, Rome, Greece, and the United States of America,[1] and if one systematically examines the frequency, length, and magnitude of these disturbances, one finds that in the long run there is no appreciable difference in this respect among the nations concerned. If anything, Russia's record is slightly less revolutionary than that of most of the nations in question. The only real difference is that of time: at a given period a given nation appears to be more revolutionary than others, whereas at another period the converse is true.

What is said of revolution applies also to *war*. Russia is generally regarded abroad as essentially belligerent, whereas the United States is thought of as eminently pacific. During the nineteenth century, to be sure, owing to the protection afforded by two broad oceans, America was somewhat more peaceful. However, if we compute in both cases all the minor wars

[1] See the systematic and, so far, the fullest data on this in my *Social and Cultural Dynamics*, Vol. III (American Book Co., 1937).

(in the case of the United States the various military expedi-
tions against Indian tribes and against some of the Latin-
American republics, such as Nicaragua, Cuba, and Haiti),
we find that in any hundred years of its history Russia shows
an average incidence of forty-six years of war as compared
with forty-eight years for the United States (or at least
seventy-seven years for the 158-year period between 1775
and 1933). As the Pacific and Atlantic Oceans become increasingly ineffective as barriers against aggression, America is
bound to grow more and more military, unless a genuine
pacification and unification of mankind is achieved. Taking
systematically all the wars in the history of Greece, Rome,
and the other main European countries, and studying them
from every significant viewpoint,[2] one discovers no fundamental difference in the relative belligerency or pacifism of
these countries. The essential difference is merely one of
time: at a given period one proves more belligerent than
another; at another period the roles are reversed.

What has been said of revolution and militarism is true of
almost every other alleged difference in national characteristics. For instance, many persons in this country used to be
convinced that the Americans were highly technical-minded,
whereas the Russians were utterly incapable of inventing or
improving machinery or even of handling machinery competently. If we compare the technological situation in the two
countries before the close of the nineteenth century, such a
conviction, to be sure, seems sound enough. Prior to that
period the United States was indeed much more creative in
this field. If, on the other hand, we systematically investigate
the facts, we find that "gadget-mindedness' is a purely *relative*
matter, depending on the particular period chosen and on
the specific circumstances of each nation during that period.

For example, when all the recorded technological inventions are taken (as 100 per cent) and the share of each nation

[2] See the facts in my *Social and Cultural Dynamics*, Vol. III.

in these inventions is computed from period to period,[3] one finds that Greek technological inventiveness was high from the sixth to the third century B.C. and very low before the sixth and after the third century B.C. Roman inventiveness was high from the first century B.C. to the third A.D., and very low before and after these centuries. Arabian inventiveness led almost the whole world in the period from 800 A.D. to about 1300, and was insignificant before and after that epoch. Among the European nations, in the ninth and tenth centuries Italy contributed 40 per cent of all the inventions, while in the nineteenth century her share shrank to from 2 to 3 per cent. Prior to the years 1726-1750 the share of the United States in this field was virtually nil; then it began slowly to increase, and between 1900 and 1908 her share was 25 per cent of the total. The share of Russia before 1876 was very negligible (between zero and 2 per cent). Thereafter it slowly increased, amounting in 1901-1908 to 3.7 per cent. In the second half of the nineteenth century the Russians made several notable technological contributions, such as the electric lamp (invented by Jablochkin two years before Thomas Edison's). But as Russia was not yet mechanically-minded, these inventions were only slightly exploited. The picture changes radically at the end of the nineteenth and throughout the twentieth century. Even those who believe in the inherent mechanical aptitude of some and inaptitude in other nations can hardly be unaware that between 1899 and 1914 and then between 1925 and 1940 the technological-industrial development of Russia made such tremendous progress that, if the present war does not destroy the chief industrial centers of Russia she will become the second most highly industrialized country in the world (the first place being occupied by this country). If they do not know this, they know at least that at the beginning of the war Russia was well supplied with

[3] Compare the detailed data on inventions in my *Social and Cultural Dynamics* (Vol. II).

planes, tanks, guns, trucks, military equipment, and with the factories necessary to produce them, in relatively larger measure than any other country except America and Germany. They may also be aware that even in this country certain outstanding inventions (including airplanes, octane gasoline, and television apparatus) are credited to Russian technologists (such as Sikorski, Ipatiev and Sworykin).

The foregoing considerations are sufficient to warrant the following conclusions: first, nobody has proved as yet that mechanical aptitude is an inherent and perennial monopoly of certain nations. Second, the assumption that the Russians are deficient in this respect is erroneous. Third, the United States developed its technological skill earlier than Russia. Fourth, after the close of the nineteenth century Russia disclosed marked technological capacity and within some forty years almost achieved second place (next to the United States). Fifth, there is scarcely any doubt that this remarkable development will continue in the future. Sixth, technological capacity is much more easily acquired than the ability to produce great literature and music or to evolve a notable religious, philosophical, or legal system.

It is undeniable that virtually all the historical nations have developed, in their respective epochs, the technology of the Stone Age, the Bronze Age, the Iron Age, and subsequent technologies — some a little earlier, others a little later. This is true of the Oriental peoples, as well — Japan, China, India, and so forth. In our special case, the extraordinary technological development of Russia since the end of the nineteenth century proves that there is not the slightest basis for claiming any essential difference in this respect between the Americans and the Russians. But not all peoples have been able to produce great literature, music, painting, or architecture, or a distinctive system of philosophy, religion, law, or ethics. (The Occident has led in this field since the fourteenth century; but prior to that century the leadership had belonged for the most part to the Oriental peoples, including the Arabs.) We should no longer delude ourselves with the belief that technological proficiency is the supreme type of cultural creativeness.

What has been said of technological talents applies in equal measure to various other alleged differences between the American and Russian mentalities. To be sure, as in any other nation, there is in Russia an undercurrent of emotionalism and mysticism, fluctuating according to circumstances. But the same is true of the United States. During the Revolution and the Civil War, as in the present war, America exhibited a high-voltage emotionalism. In view of the multiplicity of religious sects (especially in southern California), such as Jehovah's Witnesses and the Four-Square Gospel, and the vogue of revivalism (witness Billy Sunday), one is forced to conclude that in many ways American mysticism is, if anything, more pronounced than that of Russia. Observing the behavior of American crowds at football and baseball games, at political rallies, or at college reunions, one can hardly conclude that Americans are unemotional, or less emotional than Russians. On the other hand, one often hears casual remarks to the effect that although the Russians suffer, of course, from the privations of this war — hunger, cold, the loss of dear ones, etc. — yet they can bear these hardships more easily than the "civilized" nations because of their lower emotional tone and inferior sensibilities. This notion, needless to say, is as silly as the fiction of the mystic *âme slave*. The Russians suffer from hardships and losses just as much as any other people. Again, if the Russians were impractical, unrealistic, and unstable, as the proponents of the theory of the *âme slave* contend, they could scarcely have managed to create one of the greatest empires on earth; for empire building is one of the toughest tasks in the world, demanding as much practicality, realism, common sense, persistent and well-balanced effort, strength of will, and creative energy as any other human activity. Without these qualities not even a small business corporation could be organized and successfully administered. Without realism and practicality neither the heroic resistance to Hitler nor the hundreds of past victories of Russia over formidable enemies would have been possible. Without it no realistic literature and no signal accomplishments in science or technology could have been achieved. The foregoing observations should suffice to eliminate these myths once and for all from at least the realm of scientific ideas and valid theories.

2. The Congeniality of the American and Russian Mentalities

The second aspect of the thesis of this chapter — the similarity of the Russian and the American psychology — is more positive, namely, the contention that the two peoples share many fundamental mental characteristics that render their mutual relations more congenial than those which either of them sustains toward many other peoples. Foremost among these common traits are *freedom from rigid mono-nationalistic traditions and social and cultural patterns, open-mindedness and breadth of mental outlook, cosmopolitanism, and self-esteem without disparagement of others or any disposition to claim a God-given superiority over "inferior" groups.* These qualities make for *independence of thought; tolerance of the opinions, manners, and customs of others;* and *an experimental frame of mind that strives to assess the true worth of the most diverse ideas and values, regardless of their source.*

These common traits of the two nations are primarily the result of their aforesaid heterogeneous composition coupled with their "unity in diversity." Although each of the racial, ethnic, and national groups possesses its own peculiar psychology, culture, and mores, they are not mutually exclusive, owing to their constant interaction.

In their application to the United States these generalizations can hardly be challenged by Americans. Their truth is
attested by our political constitution and by our toleration
and respect for any socially harmless creed, style, pattern, or
set of mores. A case in point is our well-nigh unique toleration
of defective English, not only in informal intercourse but
even on the part of public speakers and lecturers. If a foreign
lecturer is considered to have something worth saying, and if
his English is even remotely understandable, he is listened to,
no matter how faulty his pronunciation and intonation may
be. With the exception of Russia there are few, if any, countries where one finds such forbearance. Past as well as present
immigrants to the United States could testify that this country
is possibly the only one where a newcomer does not feel a
sense of discrimination — an "unseen, subtle glass wall" which
in practically all European countries with the exception of
Russia separates him from the "old-timers." In these lands an
immigrant remains a newcomer for the rest of his life: the
"subtle glass wall" separates him very effectively from the
"native-born of native parents." In the United States this bar-
rier, as a rule, does not exist. If a foreigner has entered the
country legally, is engaged in honest work, and is not anti-
social, he ceases to be a "stranger" and becomes a full-fledged
American, being treated the same as a native-born citizen,
solely on the basis of his conduct and achievements.

Such traits are as true of Russia as of the United States.
One of the foremost of Russian writers, Dostoevski, in his
famous address on Pushkin, Russia's most eminent poet,
stressed these characteristics as typical both of Pushkin and
of the Russian nation. A few lines of this address are worth
quoting (in a free translation).

In European literature there were men of tremendous genius,
such as Shakespeare, Cervantes, and Schiller. However, one can
hardly point to a single one who had the ability of assimilating

and expressing the genius of other peoples in the same degree as
Pushkin. This ability — an inherent trait of the Russians . . . makes
Pushkin our national poet *par excellence*. The very greatest of
European poets could never express the essence of other peoples —
their soul, the unfathomable depths of their spirit, the aspirations
of their historical destiny — with the same power as Pushkin.
European poets, when they depict another than their own people,
invariably delineate it in terms of their own nationality. Shakespeare's Italians, for instance, are essentially English. But Pushkin's
Scenes from Faust, his *Miser Knight,* his ballad "There lived a poor
knight," his *Don Juan,* are so conceived that if they did not bear
his signature one would never guess that they were written by a
Russian. His *Bacchanalé in the Plague Time* bears the unmistakable
imprint of England. In his "Once wandering in a wild valley" we
not only find a literary translation of a strange and mystical book,
but glimpse in the sad and ecstatic music of its verses, into the very
soul of the northern Protestant mystic. . . . His *Imitations of the
Koran* seems to have been written by a Mohammedan, reflecting
the very spirit and sword of the Koran — the simple grandeur and
the terrible and bloody power of the Islamic faith. . . . Only in
Pushkin do we find this truly marvelous penetration of the poet's
spirit into that of other peoples. . . . In this prophetic genius of
Pushkin the Russian national soul is fully manifested. In this aspiration toward human universality, the sense of common humanity,
is found precisely Russia's outstanding characteristic. . . . Without
any discrimination, in a loving and friendly spirit, we embraced
the genius of all other peoples and nationalities. . . . Intuitively
we displayed the ability to eliminate contradictions, to reconcile
differences, thus manifesting our inclination toward a union with
all the peoples of mankind. The destiny of a Russian is indeed
pan-European and cosmopolitan. To be a genuine Russian means
to become the blood brother of all human beings. . . . In her politics, especially during the last two centuries, what has Russia
done but serve other peoples rather than herself? . . . This ideal
is demonstrated, moreover, by the whole of Russian history . . .
and by the literary genius of Pushkin. Our land may be poor, but
it was blessed by Christ, the Heavenly King, who visited it in the
guise of a slave.

In this celebrated passage Dostoevski, the seer and sage, was essentially correct. The entire texture of Russian culture and history corroborates his interpretation. *One of the historical missions of Russia has certainly been to serve and protect European and other nations — their independence, freedom, and culture — by bearing the brunt of the blows of ruthless conquerors.* This she did in respect to the Tatars: in the conquest of Russian principalities they spent their strength and could not push their devastating conquests into Europe. But Russia paid for this ordeal by more than two centuries of subjugation and spoliation. The same role Russia played, in the thirteenth century, in repelling the menace of the Teutonic Order, which was dealt a mortal blow under the leadership of Russia's valiant saint and warrior Prince Alexander Nevski. A similar function was performed in connection with the terrible incursions of the Northmen during the ninth and tenth centuries. Not without reason were they known in Europe as "the *wheep* or plague of God." By deliberately inviting some of the Northmen to become their rulers and thus absorbing their energies, the Russians served to shield Europe and Byzantium from their depredations. To multiply instances, when Charles XII of Sweden began to subjugate one country after another, Russia — after a long and costly struggle — decisively defeated him at Poltava. The same sort of mission Russia faithfully discharged vis-à-vis Napoleon, the Germans in 1914-17, and is now discharging in her epoch-making struggle with the legions of Hitler. At the cost of untold misery and bloodshed, as well as wealth, she has saved many nations in the past, just as she is now helping to save the United Nations from the menace of Nazism.

As has been suggested, the Russian nation may be compared to a vast river in which many rivulets representing a huge number of European and Asiatic peoples, nationalities, and cultures have merged. These elements are not mechanically mixed but are organically blended in a single homogeneous pattern. We have seen that throughout Russian history there has been no appreciable discrimination between races and nationalities as superior and inferior.

The Russian style in any important cultural compartment is a unity composed of various European and Asiatic elements. While the great *literature* of Russia is unmistakably indige- nous, it nevertheless possesses a European and Asiatic aroma. Russian *folk music* and *conventional music* are likewise Eurasian in the same sense. Similarly, Russian *architecture* of the past and the present is a synthesis of Byzantine, Western, and Eastern patterns. Russian museums of *painting* and *sculpture* display the personalities, the landscape, the genre scenes, and the historical events of many diverse peoples, countries, and cultures. The same is true of Russian icons, which represent a synthesis of the West and the East (including both the primitive and the most advanced cultures). The Russian *orthodox religion* exhibits the same universality: in its profound rationalism it reflects Western Christianity, while it suggests Byzantine and Eastern Christianity in its deep mysticism, reminiscent of Gregory of Nyssa, Pseudo-Dionysius, the gospel and apocalypse of Saint John, and the Oriental mystic religions in general. The same may be said of its ritual and dogmas, and the distinctive social service it has rendered to Russia.

Universal love and brotherhood, a universal and eternal Logos, ultimate reality as an infinitely manifold Godhead — these have been the leitmotif of Russia's *philosophy, religion, ethics, and charity.* Her *law* codes, again, have been "universalistic" in the sense that they have organically incorporated the basic values of the most diverse customs and common-law systems of various peoples, as well as the formal legal systems of the East and the West (including Roman law).

These traits are exhibited not only by the major compartments of Russian culture but by a host of lesser phenomena of routine experience. (To be understood properly, of course, these phenomena must be placed in the framework of the general characteristics of Russian psychology, mentality, and culture.) Here are a few typical and diagnostic facts.

Russia has *translated, published, absorbed, and keenly appreciated* the literary, artistic, philosophical, religious, ethical, legal, scholastic, and scientific works of foreign nations on a probably larger scale than any other nation. A large part of the most valuable works in these fields — American, French, German, English, Dutch, Spanish, Italian, Chinese, Hindu, etc. — have thus become more familiar to educated Russians than to the intelligentsia of almost any other land. This explains the oft observed fact of the broadmindedness of educated Russians and eminence of Russia's cultural contributions in the fields of literature, philosophy, and science. Russia has known more of the cultural creations of the world than any foreign nation has known either of Russian culture or of foreign cultures in general. Hence she has tended to remain an enigma to outsiders, whereas outside cultures have by no means been a mystery to her. Herein we discern again the broad, universalistic soul of Russia.

In a slightly different form this characteristic of *striving for universality permeates also the American culture.* This country has become an asylum for the refugees of other countries to an extent unparalleled elsewhere. It has admitted to professional, governmental, and other high positions probably a much greater proportion of foreigners of all nationalities than has any other land. In recent times, moreover, the United States has been absorbing the cultural values of other countries (Latin America, Europe, Asia, and Africa) to an extent rivaled possibly only by Russia. In this respect the parallel of the universal soul of the United States with that of Russia is rather striking.

This parallelism is disclosed in many other ways. It was Russia which initiated, through the late Czar Nicholas II, the

Hague International Court of Arbitration as a means of preventing war, just as it was the United States which, through President Wilson, initiated the League of Nations as an instrument of maintaining world peace. The same aspiration toward universalism and human brotherhood is revealed by the frequent instances of sympathetic idealistic participation, and sometimes even of leadership, on the part of Russians and Americans aimed at the amelioration of social conditions in other countries. A number of Russian intellectuals (such as Pechorin in the first part of the nineteenth century) were converted to Catholicism because the Catholic Church appeared to them as the power best suited for attaining this humanitarian objective. Other intellectuals (like Vyroubov and De-Roberti), became the world leaders of the post-Contean humanistic positivism, because this positivism, with its religion of humanity seemed to them the most potent force for the realization of that purpose. A still larger number of Russians, including Bakunin and Kropotkin, and those associated with the First, Second and Third International, identified themselves with international revolutionary movements, fighting and sometimes dying (like Turgenev's Rudin) in the service of various countries in which they did not have any specific personal or national interest. Such internationalism is a further manifestation of the universalism and cosmopolitan 'pan-humanism" which we have been discussing. From this standpoint even the recent Russian Communism, with its Third International, displays — perhaps in a perverted form — the same aspiration for universal justice and brotherhood. Although Marxism and Communism were invented in Europe, and were in no sense an original Russian product, nevertheless it was in Russia that they first found direct, practical application on a large scale. Through her willingness to test these dangerous schemes of social reconstruction Russia served the cause of all mankind by showing the terrific price to be paid for such an experiment. Her own martyrdom thus proved a warning and a source of instruction to the rest of the world.

A similar propensity is disclosed by America's unique role in serving the cause of liberty, charity, religion, and a host of other values throughout almost the entire world. During and after the First World War it has played the leading part in relief activities (including the maintenance of food stations) during famines, wars, and like emergencies; in the founding of hospitals, schools, and missions; and in the financing and administering of various other beneficent projects — causes in which Americans have had no personal or national interest apart from idealism and striving for human brotherhood. All this affords a close parallel to the disposition of the Russians to "meddle" in matters which from egoistic or nationalistic motives do not concern them. Both nations thus appear in the light of "crusading Don Quixotes." Only the Jews and possibly the English exhibit this propensity to a comparable degree.

As additional evidence of the psychological affinity of the two peoples may be cited the mutual impact of their respective cultures. (This will be discussed at length in a later chapter.) Here it is sufficient to say that the interpenetration of their cultural values has been at once prodigious and fruitful. Each culture and society has enriched the other to an extent far greater than most people realize.

For the present we shall continue our comparison of the two cultures and societies by discussing those institutions and values which are regarded as diametrically opposite. Foremost among these are the social and political institutions of Russia and America. Let us now turn to their consideration.

CHAPTER FOUR

RUSSIAN AND AMERICAN SOCIAL INSTITUTIONS

1. *Their Democratic Nature*

The next important similarity of the two countries consists in the essentially democratic structure of their basic socio-cultural institutions. In regard to the United States this statement will not be questioned. But in application to prerevolutionary Russia it will undoubtedly sound to many paradoxical if not unbelievable. The autocracy and absolutism of the Czarist regime will at once be brought forward as incontrovertible evidence of the fallacy of the statement. This so-called autocratic Czarist regime has acted as a screen which has hidden from foreigners the truly democratic constitution of the basic social institutions of Russia — in pre-Tatar and post-Tatar times, and especially in the second part of the nineteenth century, not to mention the present post-revolutionary period. The superficiality of foreign reporters and "experts" on Russia is responsible, moreover, for an excessive exaggeration of the autocracy of the Czarist regime itself.

The term "democracy" is a word of many diverse meanings, some of which are actually opposed. Can a country practicing slavery, like the United States before the Civil War, be called democratic? Can a country marked by rigid religious intolerance, like colonial Massachusetts, be called democratic? Can a country in which (legally or actually) the higher positions are monopolized to a great extent by a hereditary or semi-hereditary upper class, as in most of colonial America and to some extent in present-day England, be regarded as democratic? Can a country possessing subjugated colonies, exploited and disfranchised in many respects, like colonial Great Britain, France, or Italy, or with a vast substratum of slaves and semislaves, like ancient Athens, be deemed democratic? Can a country in which the central government regiments, controls, and administers most of the economic and other sociocultural relations of its citizens, like the contemporary United States or Great Britain, not to mention the openly dictatorial countries such as Russia or Germany, be termed democratic? Finally, can a country in which there is an enormous contrast in standards of living, in wealth and poverty, its citizens ranging from the poverty-stricken unemployed to multimillionaires, be thought of as democratic?

These questions are raised, not for rhetorical purposes, but to suggest that "democracy" and "democratic" are terms which circulate widely on the intellectual market without any definite meaning. Hence it would be well to take, one by one, the fundamental social institutions of both countries and indicate specifically their essential characteristics, past and present. The reader may then decide for himself whether the term "democratic" is or is not applicable to them, and whether or not they have been parallel in the two cases.

2. *The Family*

Let us begin with the basic institution of the family. The American family — in its structure; in its relationship of husband and wife, parents and children; in its property relations — is believed to be essentially democratic at the present time. In the past it was, like the dominant type of the European family, more patriarchal, and hence less democratic in the modern sense.

What has been the character of the Russian family? It has undergone, as in other countries, several notable changes in the course of Russian history, from the ninth to the twentieth century. At some periods it was patriarchal. But whatever forms it has assumed, *it has been as democratic as any of the European family institutions if not more so.*

To many this statement will appear incredible; yet it is quite accurate. Let us take the status and mutual relations of men and women, husband and wife, parents and children, and then the structure of family property, as the most important elements of which the Russian as well as any family institution is made up.

The Status of Women in Russia. During the last few months I have read two articles by a *New York Times* reporter in Moscow and several articles by alleged "experts" on Russia, as well as a couple of books, and have listened to an indefinite number of radio talks, all of which have unanimously stressed the profound contrast in the position of Russian women before and after the Revolution. According to these statements, Russian women before the Revolution were in a position similar to that of the inmates of Oriental harems — shut off from the rest of the world within their *terem,* wholly subject to men, deprived of all participation in public, governmental, professional, and other functions. *After* the Revolution, according to these "experts," the situation changed radically,—nay, fantastically — with the result that Russian women are now completely emancipated, participating as equal partners with men in all public activities, not excluding even war.

It is unnecessary to point out that, so far as the prerevolutionary status of women is concerned, the picture is false. If these writers and commentators possessed an elementary knowledge of Russian history, they could hardly have uttered such nonsense. They would have known that as early as the ninth or tenth centuries a series of women (such as the Princesses Olga, Rogneda, and so forth) played a very important part as rulers, in social and public activities, or as champions of their independence and dignity as wives. During subsequent centuries Russian women played as notable a role in social, governmental, political, and cultural activities as women in any European country. Russian women occupied the highest government positions, such as that of the president of a republic (for instance, Marfa Posadnitza in the fifteenth-century Novgorod Republic); of an empress in her own right (for example, Catherina I, Anna Ioannovna, Elizabeth, and Catherine the Great); or of a powerful ruler and a leader in a political cabal against a rival Czar, such as the Czarina Sophia, a sister of Peter the Great, in her competition with him for the throne. One might cite a formidable list of women revolutionary leaders against the Czarist regime (such as S. Perovskaia, Vera Sassoulitch, and K. Breshkovskaia); of women like Morozova (a noblewoman of Muscovy) and the wives of many of the Decembrists, who took a leading part in various struggles for religious and political freedom; of military heroines like Nadezhda Durova, the heroine of the war of 1812 against Napoleon; of famous scientists, such as the mathematician Sophia Kovalevskaia; of distinguished novelists, dramatists, poets, musicians, painters, sculptors, and architects; and a host of women who have occupied less eminent positions in connection with political, governmental, and professional activities, social-welfare work, and the like.

The aforesaid "experts" should at least have taken the pains to acquaint themselves with the Russian civil law that defines the structure of the family and the position of the wife; or with the catalogues of Russian universities and colleges, noting the large number of names of women professors in even the foremost prerevolutionary institutions of higher learning for men. Again, they might have glanced at the imposing array of names of doctors and lawyers, editors and journalists, reporters, columnists, merchants, and even directors and managers of banks and other business firms. They would have discovered that in prerevolutionary Russia, in the leading universities for men, there were more women professors (including full professors of distinction) than in contemporary American male and co-educational universities. They would have learned, moreover, that, side by side with coeducational institutions, prerevolutionary Russia possessed first-class women's universities, colleges, and other schools. Again, they would have observed that the proportion of women in the Russian medical profession before the Revolution was probably much larger than its counterpart in the United States in the year 1943. In all these varied fields of activity the proportion of women in the prerevolutionary Russia of the close of the nineteenth century and the early years of the twentieth century was certainly no smaller than in the United States prior to the present war. The same is true of women workers in factories and mills and in many other trades and crafts, as well as in agriculture. This means that before the Revolution the women of Russia were emancipated as fully as those of any other land, including America, and probably more so than in most European countries.

Finally, if a foreigner were to attend the meetings held by the peasants at their village "town halls" for the discussion and decision of their common affairs, he would see not a few women participating in the discussion and voting on the same footing as the men.

In all this, as well as in many other respects, the Revolution did not introduce anything new, merely continuing vital trends of Russian history that had existed long before the Revolution. The complete emancipation and equality of women in present-day Russia is simply the fulfillment of a long historical process. The Revolution applied, so to speak, the finishing touches to a movement that had essentially reached its culmination in the prerevolutionary Russia of the twentieth century. This proves that in this respect Russia has always been as democratic as any of the Western countries, and more democratic than most of them.

The Marital Status in the Russian Family. This conclusion is re-enforced by a study of the structure of the Russian family as a union of husband and wife. Here are some salient points which show clearly that the family was a more democratic institution throughout the history of Russia than in most European countries during the same period. First, while a certain amount of polygamy existed among the Russian tribes before the introduction of Christianity (in the ninth century), it rapidly disappeared thereafter. Although under the Tatar dominion, and (in Muscovy) from the fifteenth to the seventeenth century, the sequestration of women was practiced to a certain extent, such confinement was relatively slight compared with that of women in western European countries during the same period. Second, the free consent of parties entering the marriage relation was a general rule even in ancient times; and after the accession of Peter the Great it was required by law, even in regard to the serfs, whose masters were forbidden to compel the parties to marry against their wishes.

Third, unions of Russians and non-Russians, and of members of the Russian Orthodox Church and Roman Catholics, Protestants, or other Christians, were permitted. Only intermarriage between members of the Russian Orthodox Church and non-Christians was prohibited. However, non-Orthodox Christians (such as Protestants) were allowed to marry Mohammedans or Jews. These limitations (which were quite common throughout Europe, and more drastic than in Russia) were not motivated by racial or national considerations but rested exclusively on religious grounds. As soon as a non-Christian was converted, all such restrictions disappeared. By the early twentieth century virtually every prohibition in this field had been abolished.

Fourth, although (with the exception of the destructive period of the Revolution) the incidence of divorce was very low in comparison with that of other Western countries, nevertheless freedom of divorce was permitted by law to a larger extent than in most European lands, and — what is still more important — the rights of the wife in this respect were substantially identical with those of the husband, whereas in the majority of Western nations the position of the husband was ordinarily much more privileged than that of the wife. As early as the Muscovy period the legal grounds for divorce (including that of mutual consent) were more liberal than in most European countries. Later on there were some slight fluctuations in these grounds; but throughout all the subsequent centuries divorce was more readily obtained than in most other Western lands. Since the accession of Peter the Great, in particular, the equality of the two partners in respect to divorce has been the rule — both theoretically and actually— whether the ground has been adultery, sexual impotence, crime, the disappearance of one of the parties for more than five years, or the like.

Fifth, as regards personal and property rights, Russian law and practice (especially since the time of Peter the Great) have always insisted upon full equality and, concerning the tenure of property, complete independence. This status contrasts sharply with that of the Teutonic family, where from the earliest times the wife was almost wholly subject to the authority and stewardship of her husband (*mundium*), losing all her property rights (even over the property which she had owned prior to her marriage), and where the husband constituted the sole representative of the family in its economic and other relationships with the rest of society; and it contrasts only less strikingly with the marital status of the wife in the majority of European countries, in which, among other things, her economic autonomy has been notably limited until quite recently. The guiding principle of Russian law and practice in this respect has been that economically the two parties are equal and independent. Hence the wife remains after marriage the sole owner of everything she had before marriage or acquired subsequently.[1]

[1] There is one qualification of this generalization that should be noted, namely, that when the parties belonged to different "orders" — say, the husband was a member of the nobility and the wife belonged to one of the lower classes — the privileges of the husband were shared by the wife, who automatically became

To sum up, the Russian family, as a union of husband and wife, has long been more democratic than that of most of the Western countries. In this respect, once again, the Revolution (if we ignore its destructive phase) did not introduce anything new, but merely continued a long-standing trend in the field of domestic life. That at the present time the wife enjoys a status fully equal to that of her husband is well known even to the "experts," and requires no corroboration.

In spite of (or perhaps *because* of?) the fundamental equality of the status of husband and wife, the Russian family (apart from the destructive phase of the Revolution in the years 1918-1934) has been *notably stable*. The percentage of divorce and separation has been distinctly low in comparison with that prevailing in most of the Western countries — particularly in the United States. During the destructive period of the Revolution, to be sure, when the Communist government deliberately attempted to undermine monogamous marriage and the family as the cornerstone of private property, the stability of the family sharply declined, divorces exhibiting an extraordinarily high rate. However, by the middle of the thirties this tendency had been checked; and at present the Russian family once more ranks among the stablest in the entire world.

The Parent-Children Relationship in the Russian Family. With slight modifications, what has been said of the husband-wife relationship applies also to the relations between parents and children. Legally and actually these relations in prerevolutionary Russia were as democratic as in any Western country; and — apart from the destructive period of the Revolution, the family, as a union of parents and children, has

a "noble," whereas when the wife belonged to the nobility and the husband did not, the wife's status was not extended to her husband. Similarly, any privileges acquired by the husband *after* marriage were shared by his wife, though the converse was not true. This difference, it is readily seen, operated to the advantage of the wife and to the disadvantage of her mate.

always been as strong and stable an institution in Russia as in any other land.

In the remote past the Russian family was patriarchal in character; and even as late as the second half of the nineteenth century it was not uncommon for the family to consist of some twenty to fifty members, representing three different generations living together in the same home. Thereafter it generally consisted merely of the parents and children, including one or more married children. The separation of the children from their parents has occurred less frequently and at a later age than in the United States and many other countries.

Under the strictly patriarchal regime the parents exercised wide authority over the children, though hardly the unlimited authority of the ancient Greek, Roman, and early Teutonic *pater familias;* for in Russia the father never possessed the right of life or death over his children. The relations of parents and children — legally and actually — were always assumed to be "natural," "moral," and "social" — that is, free and spontaneous, the rights and duties of each party redounding to the benefit alike of parents and children and of society at large. The law code of 1550 explicitly prohibited selling children into servitude; and the edicts of Peter the Great limited the right of parents to hire their children out for a longer period than five years and forbade them to relegate them to a monastery or to compel them to marry against their wishes. The mutual duties of parents and children — such as the duty of the parents to care for their children, to educate them, and the like, and the obligation of the children to respect their parents, to support them in their old age, and so forth — were typical of the self-respecting family of any civilized country. The disciplinary measures which the law of prerevolutionary Russia permitted parents in respect to recalcitrant children were highly restricted so far as punitive action was concerned, the maximum being a court petition envisaging a jail sentence up to a period of four months. But the actual practice fell so far short of this that even many lawyers were not aware that the penal code contained such an article. For any cruel or unwarranted treatment of their children the parents were held strictly responsible and could be punished. Again, if parents were deprived of their civil rights because of crime, the children did not share this deprivation. Moreover, as in the case of the wife vis-à-vis her husband, the children's property rights were amply protected.

To sum up. All in all, the Russian family, as a union of parents and children, has proved — morally, socially, and legally — as noble, sound, and stable as that of any of the Western countries. On the whole it has been rather more democratic than the dominant type of family in many Western lands. It has been relatively free from the excesses which often mar such relations: those of undue parental authority, on the one hand, and of premature freedom and cessation of responsibility toward their parents on the part of the children, on the other; of a mutual attitude marked by exaggerated formalism, legalism, and calculation, including the attitude toward pecuniary matters, or one vitiated by erratic and unstable spontaneity. As has been said, the Communist revolution temporarily disorganized the family; but after the middle thirties the latter recovered its prerevolutionary characteristics (cf. Chapter Nine). In this, as in other respects, the Revolution eliminated what was already moribund, perpetuating the vital trends of the Russian family.

3. *Russian Provincial, Local, and Municipal Self-Government.*

Peasant Self-Government: Political and Economic Democracy. If we glance at Russia's prerevolutionary provincial, local, and municipal self-government, we are once again impressed with the essentially democratic character of its institutions. Let us begin with peasant self-government.

After the abolition of serfdom in 1861, before the elimination of the peasant *mir* and *obschina* (in the twentieth century), when the status of peasants was placed on an equal footing with that of the citizenry in general, the peasants managed their own affairs (including the choice, by popular vote, of the county chief and secretary, or the *volostnoi starshina* and *volostnoi pisar*) by means of meetings, held in their villages or county seats, similar to the system of town-hall democracy in New England. Moreover, the discussion and voting were shared on an equal basis by the men and women. At the turn of the century this system of peasant self-government began to be supervised and controlled by the central government through the appointment of special agents (*zemski nachalnik*), who were abolished, however, after 1905.

The democratic character of the system in question was much more deep-seated than appears on the surface. The *mir* and *obschina* represented not merely a political unity but an economic collectivity; for the land belonged not to this or that individual but to the entire village or community. One of the reasons for this arrangement was the desire to prevent the alienation of peasant property, the pauperization of the peasants, and the increase of landless peasant-tenants and laborers. Every inhabitant of a given village was granted a portion of the land for purposes of cultivation and use; but no individual was given a title deed, the ownership being vested in the entire peasant community. Each peasant received a share of the land in proportion to the size of his family. Furthermore, since the land varied in quality, he was allotted a certain amount of good, medium-grade, and poor land, as well as his proper quota of the common pasture, and of grasslands for hay making. Since some peasant families tended to grow, whereas others declined in size, from time to time — say every second or fifth year — the peasants made a redistribution of the village land to conform to these changes in the size of their families.

In addition to constituting a political and economic democracy, this peasant system, represented by the *mir* and the *obschina,* was a familistic collectivity in which the entire community undertook to care for its members not only in respect to an equitable reapportionment of the land but also in respect to mutual aid. For instance, it furnished poor relief. Again, if a peasant wanted to build a house, his neighbors assisted him free of charge. Upon the death of a peasant the whole community attended his funeral obsequies. Furthermore, before the introduction of *zemstvo,* "ministerial," and denominational schools, the *mir* engaged teachers and established schools at its own expense.

The Co-operative Movement. This genuinely communal system explains the extraordinary success of the *co-operative movement* prior to the Revolution. Most foreigners do not realize that this movement — embracing consumers, producers, and others — was more highly developed in prerevolutionary Russia than in any other country. Its membership exceeded thirteen million; and its capital, in the early twentieth century, amounted to hundreds of millions. In addition to their purely economic functions, the Russian co-operatives increasingly engaged in such cultural activities as the establishment and maintenance of schools and institutes, newspapers and magazines, and the political, scientific, and ethical leadership of the masses. From the standpoint of the quality of its economic and cultural services, the Russian prerevolutionary co-operative movement was certainly second to none in the world. Quantitatively it was without a rival. In contradistinction to the contemporary governmental pseudo-cooperatives, it was wholly voluntary. In itself it amply demonstrates the profoundly democratic propensities of the Russian people. The extraordinary success of this co-operative organization was due largely to the *mir* and *obschina* and other communal and collective institutions. It is to be regretted that during the destructive phase of the Revolution these free co-operatives were replaced by compulsory, bureaucratically controlled pseudo-co-operatives. Fortunately, however, they are beginning to revive, and they will doubtless play an important role in the future.

Provincial and Municipal Self-Government. Not only the peasantry but all other classes in prerevolutionary Russia possessed a remarkable institution of county or provincial self-government known as the *zemstvo*. Introduced after the liberation of the serfs in 1861, the *zemstvo* became one of the most fruitful institutions of local self-government in the world. Owing to a conjunction of favorable circumstances, the character of its personnel[2] and its success in discharging both its administrative and its cultural functions proved so notable — so free from the political corruption and other vices frequently associated with local administration — that it cannot be too highly praised. During the fifty-five years or so of its existence the *zemstvo* constituted one of the foremost educational and cultural forces in Russia. (Incidentally, it served as the prototype for the American system of county agents.) Although many similar institutions in other countries may appear, on the basis of their written constitutions, to be more liberal and more radically democratic, it is doubtful whether the *zemstvo* has been surpassed from the standpoint either of its social ideals or of its actual performance.

At the close of the nineteenth century, before its overthrow, the decadent Czarist government began to intermeddle with the activities of the *zemstvo*, with a view to controlling and curbing them, just as it did in the case of peasant self-government and other institutions. Nevertheless, these attempts of the central government proved largely abortive up to the time of the Communist Revolution. Since the decline of the destructive phases of the Revolution there is good reason to believe

---

[2] Not only the personnel of the *zemstvo* but also that of the courts established by the signal reforms of 1861 was distinguished by an extraordinary degree of practical idealism.

that the *zemstvo* (or its equivalent) will re-emerge as an indispensable instrument of self-government.

Finally, prerevolutionary Russia enjoyed also a good system of *municipal self-government* (somewhat inferior, to be sure, to the *zemstvo* in its administrative and cultural functions), based on the suffrage of the more prosperous elements of the city population. The central government, during its period of decline, endeavored to take this too under its control, but without any appreciable degree of success. With the advent of the Bolshevist Revolution, municipal self-government was unfortunately replaced by the dictatorial bureaucracy of the Communist party.

The foregoing discussion clearly indicates that such basic Russian institutions as the family and the systems of peasant, provincial, local, and municipal self-government were truly democratic — probably more democratic than those of most of the Western countries during the same period. Before turning to a consideration of the relative autocracy of the central government, let us view briefly the legal and judicial system and the aristocracy as they existed prior to the Revolution, particularly after the reforms of 1861 and the following years.

4. *The Russian Legal and Judicial System*

Space does not permit even a brief résumé of the history of the Russian legal and judicial system. Most of the ideas current in foreign lands respecting these institutions are utterly erroneous, if not fantastic. Russian law and justice during the past centuries have, needless to say, been by no means perfect, but they have been hardly inferior to the corresponding institutions of other countries, and in several respects they have been sounder and more humanitarian. For instance, if we consider the criminal law, we find that about the middle of the eighteenth century, during the reign of the Empress Elizabeth, capital punishment was abolished for all crimes except attempts on the life of the Czar and immediate members of his family. This fact in itself exposes the fallacy of the conception of Russian law and justice, prevalent abroad, as something barbarous and cruel.[3]

The civil and criminal laws instituted by the reforms of 1861 were about as humane, democratic, progressive, and effective as any civil and criminal code in the West and in several respects were even more just and democratic. While they embodied certain peculiar features unfamiliar outside Russia, these peculiarities, far from constituting defects, were merely adaptations essential to meet the exigencies of Russian social conditions. Similar divergences, moreover, are found in the civil and criminal codes of France, Germany, and Italy and in the codes, statutes, and common law of the Anglo-Saxon countries. In contradistinction to Anglo-Saxon law, which still remains uncodified and still depends to a large extent upon the temperament of a given judge, Russian law was codified long ago, and underwent a fundamental recodification at the hands of Speranski at the beginning of the nineteenth century. Subsequently, from time to time, it was revised here and there, to conform to altered conditions, and came to

[3] A rather striking phenomenon in this connection is the extremely small number of cases of capital punishment typical of Russia during normal years. During the period 1881-1905 the average annual number of executions ranged from 9.6 to 18.6 — a figure often exceeded in many single states of the American Union. The rate rose sharply during the revolution of 1905-1908 and after the year 1917, attaining during 1918-1922 the fantastic proportions of approximately 150,000 a year. But such an increase is typical of all countries under similar emergency conditions. The dissemination of false information abroad concerning the alleged cruelties of the Czarist regime at the end of the nineteenth century and in the early years of the twentieth century is attributable primarily to Russian revolutionary propaganda. On the basis of my experience as a university professor of criminal law and procedure, and as a prisoner (on three occasions) under the old regime, I consider that the chief defect of the decadent Romanoff system lay not in its brutality (which was relatively negligible) but, rather, in its stupidity and incapacity — even impotence.

incorporate most of the modern reforms — such as juvenile-court procedure and the provision of model reformatories for prisoners — which one finds in other Western countries.

Conversely, the criminal code of Soviet Russia enacted in 1926, during the destructive period of the Revolution, like the actual administration of justice under this system, represented a decided retrogression in the direction of barbarity. The number of crimes punishable by death (the official term in the Soviet code is "the highest degree of punishment") increased enormously in comparison with the prerevolutionary code, as did the severity of the penalties meted out; and many perfectly innocuous social activities were branded as crimes. In actual practice the Soviet "justice" of that period was one of the cruelest in the entire history of penology, marked by the indiscriminate butchery of at least 600,000 persons in the years 1918-1922 alone. However, similar blood-thirstiness is characteristic of all profound revolutions, from the earliest recorded revolution in Egypt (*ca.* 2500 B.C.) and those of ancient Greece and Rome to the internal convulsions of modern Europe. Since the passing of the destructive phase of the Soviet Revolution there has been a progressive tendency to re-establish a system of judicial procedure bearing some semblance of real justice.

As a student of law I know that however good a system of law and justice may look on paper, its merits may be largely nullified by the way it is administered by its human agents — namely, judges, lawyers, and attorneys. The question therefore arises, what kind of judges, lawyers, and prosecuting attorneys did prerevolutionary Russia possess? After the judicial reforms of 1861 they were among the very best in the world. Here again, as in the case of the *zemstvo*, the personnel represented a rare combination of genuine idealism, excellent technical training, and a deep sense of practical realism. Animated by a desire to render judicial social service as fairly and efficiently as possible, the rank and file of Russian judges, prosecuting attorneys, and lawyers between 1861 and 1917 were guided by standards as high as those of the American Supreme Court or of English judges at their best. The procedure of the Russian courts of that period was not only just and competent but distinctly humane and idealistic. Corruption, bribery, cynical manipulation of legal technicalities, partiality, and similar defects were reduced to the minimum.[4]

The lofty standards of the personnel were due, as I have suggested, to an idealistic *élan* that swept over Russian society in the period of the notable reforms of 1861 and the following years. Its technical competency is attributable to the rigid training of prospective jurists in the universities. This training (which the writer underwent in his study of law) was as solid as that of students in American law schools, and decidedly broader in scope. In the latter the general theory of law, the history of law (including Roman law), comparative law, and a number of other fundamental disciplines are relatively neglected in comparison with the curriculum of the Russian-university law schools. In addition to this solid theoretical training, prospective Russian jurists (judges, lawyers, and attorneys) had to undergo a period of practical training similar to that of medical practitioners before they were fully qualified to perform their judicial and legal functions. Finally, all candidates were subjected to a severe test, not only respecting their technical proficiency, but also concerning their personal integrity and general fitness. All these factors account for the exceptionally high standard of the Russian legal profession throughout the period in question.

The system was as truly democratic as any, the closest parallel being the English system. *Justices of the peace were*

---

[4] This generalization applies strictly to the regular courts of justice — not to the administrative decisions of the agents of the central government, especially in the treatment of political offenders. The machinery and functioning of the administrative police and gendarmerie were in many ways thoroughly corrupt.

elected, as in England and in this country, but only from among persons possessed of the requisite legal and moral qualifications. The judges of the higher courts, including the Senate (a body akin to the United States Supreme Court), were appointed from among candidates recommended by the bar and the most authoritative justices as not only possessing all the necessary qualifications but as the very best material available. Their appointment, like that of the English justices and the justices of our Supreme Court, was for life; and they could not be removed save for crime and other behavior incompatible with their high calling. This made their position independent of the central government, political parties, economic pressure, and other factors that often interfere with the proper discharge of the duties of a judge. In all these respects the justices of the higher courts enjoyed a status very similar to that of English justices and those of the United States Supreme Court. All in all, the courts in Russia were freer from political pressure than they are in this country with the exception of the Supreme Court.

Finally, *all the serious crimes (or felonies) were tried in Russia, as in this country, by jury,* and the jurymen were selected as democratically as in this country. The jury decided the question of guilt, the judge determining only the amount of the punishment if the defendant was found guilty. Moreover, the discretion of the judge was less arbitrary than in the United States, since the Russian criminal codes explicitly prescribed the minimum and maximum penalty, with a rather comprehensive enumeration of the principal aggravating and mitigating circumstances. In addition, in grave crimes the penalty was determined not by *one* judge but by *three or more* (as in our Supreme Court).

On the whole, in criminal as well as in civil matters the population of Russia, including the poorest classes, had as good a chance of obtaining justice as in this country, and the judge discharged his duties as faithfully and equitably as anywhere else.

The foregoing evidence demonstrates the absurdity of current opinion abroad concerning the Russian prerevolutionary legal and judicial profession. Although this admirable institution was demolished during the early years of the Revolution, being supplanted by the arbitrary and bloody Communist system of pseudo-justice, nevertheless, as I have pointed out, such a resurgence of barbarity under the impact of a major revolution is not peculiar to Russia. A return to the prerevolutionary system of justice is already in evidence, and the trend is bound to continue until this precious heritage of Russian culture is fully restored, if not in its letter, at least in its spirit and its essential nature.

5. *The Russian Aristocracy and Bourgeoisie (or Middle Classes)*

The prevalent opinion about the Russian upper and middle classes current among foreigners is that they were castelike orders, closed to persons born in the lower classes, and therefore thoroughly undemocratic. This notion is erroneous, particularly concerning the period after the reforms of 1861.

In regard to the *aristocracy,* I have already pointed out that from the standpoint of national and ethnic groups it was always less self-contained than the aristocracy of other Western countries. The same is substantially true as regards the infiltration of the lower classes of the population. Peter the Great's edict of the so-called "Table of Ranks" rendered it even more accessible than the British or American aristocracy. The Table of Ranks divided the free population into fourteen classes, and established as the basis for promotion, the criteria of *individual ability and achievement, regardless of race, birth, social status, or any other condition.* To quote a Russian historian (Platonov): "All men, whether aristocrats or plebeians, started at the lowest rungs of the ladder with the possibility of reaching the highest. The order of such promotion was clearly defined by a 'Table of Ranks' (1722). It divided all the government positions into fourteen ranks, or *chins*. The principle of individual merit now triumphed over aristocratic lineages." After this revolutionary law the nobility and aristocracy became less and less a matter of blood and caste and more and more a stratum of capable state officials recruited from all classes. For instance, the son of a peasant or laborer who graduated from a university ceased to be a peasant or laborer and became automatically "ennobled." The same may be said of many other avenues of promotion from the ranks of the lower classes. In all these respects the Russian nobility — including its highest ranks — was more open to talented members of the lower classes than even the English nobility and aristocracy. If one examines the genealogies of the Russian nobility as it existed before the Revolution, and the social origin of the high governmental officials in the nineteenth and early twentieth centuries, one discovers that only a small proportion of the nobles possessed conspicuous aristocratic antecedents, the majority consisting of families or individuals with only one or two generations — if any — of noble ancestors. This process went on at an accelerating pace as we pass from the eighteenth to the twentieth century. In the sense of constituting an aristocracy of merit the Russian aristocracy was at least as democratic as that of most of the Western countries, if not more so.

Side by side with this phenomenon the privileges and fortunes of the aristocracy and nobility tended rapidly to decline throughout the nineteenth and early twentieth century. The liberation of the serfs dealt the upper classes a hard blow. Thereafter the main source of wealth of the nobility — the land — rapidly passed into the hands of peasantry and other classes, so that on the eve of the Revolution only some 8 to 10 per cent of all the cultivated land remained in its hands. Other privileges were progressively lost through the equalization of the rights of the citizenry in general and through the rise of the wealthy bourgeoisie. The Revolution found the nobility impoverished and relatively powerless, playing a role far more modest than that of the new bourgeoisie. Indeed, it was already moribund — the mere shadow of its former self. The Revolution accordingly simply administered the *coup de grâce*.

As to the *bourgeoisie, or middle classes,* in prerevolutionary Russia, in spite of a vigorous quantitative and qualitative development after 1861, at the time of the Revolution they had unfortunately not yet become numerically one of the most powerful classes in the state. Hence they could not check the Revolution. From the qualitative standpoint, however, the developing bourgeoisie — especially the professions — displayed all the positive merits of vigor, initiative, industry, public service, social responsibility, and talent.

The Russian business class of the end of the nineteenth and the beginning of the twentieth century reminds one strongly of the enterprising American business of the recent past, that of Carnegie, the Rockefellers, and similar economic empire-builders. To this class Russia is largely indebted for the rapid development of its industries and its resources, which, as we shall see, quadrupled within the brief period of 1890-1913 (increasing from 1.5 billion rubles in 1890 to 6 billion rubles in 1913), and was reflected in a rising standard of living. To this class it is likewise indebted for various social services, animated by a spirit of public philanthropy and generosity: the founding and financing of private universities and schools; scientific research institutes; museums; theaters, operas, and kindred artistic enterprises; newspapers and magazines; various religious and philanthropic institutions; and even revolutionary movements. The Liberal, Social Democratic, Social Revolutionary, and Communist parties and their leaders were substantially assisted through the financial contributions of the new Russian bourgeoisie, whose progressivism and liberalism were manifested also by the establishment of its own political parties, such as that of the "Constitutional Democrats" and the "Business Party." After 1905, although it constituted only a small proportion of the total population, its increasing influence was evinced by the fact that in the first *Duma,* or parliament, its representatives formed one of the strongest parties, and in the second and the third *Duma* came to exercise controlling power.

To sum up. Economically, socially, politically, culturally, and psychologically, the Russian bourgeoisie was very closely akin to the American business class. As for the other elements of the middle class — especially the *intelligentsia* and the *professional* groups — their talent, ability, technical competence, and deep spirit of idealism and of social service are well known even outside of Russia. The Russian artist, musician, writer, journalist, scientist, teacher, scholar, doctor, lawyer, engineer, inventor, etc., are justly esteemed and praised even abroad. The Russian term *intelligentsia* actually became a synonym for a group highly intellectual, well trained, and competent, possessing conspicuous moral and social integrity and an altruistic spirit of social service — the embodiment of a democratic spirit of aspiration.

The only shortcoming of the Russian professional class was its small size. Owing to this factor, it was, like the business class, unable to avert most of the destructive activities of the first phase of the Revolution. In the effort to prevent the terrorism and bestiality of the Communist rule a considerable portion of its members perished, being executed, imprisoned, banished, or deprived of their means of subsistence. It performed its duty faithfully. If it did not fully succeed in its task, this was simply because of the overwhelming odds with which it had to contend.

Thus, from the peasantry to the aristocracy the social structure and institutions of Russia were, before the Revolution, as democratic as those of most of the countries of the West. There remains for us to consider the central government, or Czarist regime, and to inquire whether it was, in fact, something Oriental in its absolutism and autocracy. The results will be instructive and enlightening.

6. *The Russian Central Government*

The principal stages in the evolution of the central political regime may be summed up as follows.

The political organization of the Russian principalities and republics prior to the Tatar invasion — from the ninth to the thirteenth century — was as democratic as in any European country. Several principalities, such as Novgorod and Pskov, were explicitly republics, with a democratic system of folk-moots (*vetsche*) somewhat similar to the town-hall self-government of colonial America. Other principalities, though not definitely republics, were neither monarchies nor autocracies. Their ruler was in most cases a sort of hired "principality manager" (like our "city managers"), entrusted primarily with military defence and certain other administrative functions, and employed and discharged by the citizens of the principality. In other words, the prince was elective, and his status was purely contractual. The only limitation upon the freedom of this contract was that the ruler had to be chosen from among the descendants of the family of the first Russian prince, Rurik, a Northman voluntarily called in by the people. All the important affairs of such a principality were decided at the *vetsche*, or meeting of the full-fledged citizens. Thus none of the princes was a real monarch—much less an autocrat.

Occasionally some of the princes managed to play the role of fairly autocratic bosses, but their power as such was *de facto* rather than legal, due either to exceptional ability and prestige or to successful machinations (like those of certain contemporary bosses of Tammany Hall). What is still more important, the princes and other persons wielding authority did not rule arbitrarily but had to conform to the norms embodied in the law codes. As early as the first half of the eleventh century the principality of Kiev enacted the code known as *Russkaia Pravda* (or *Russian Truth*), whose humane character placed it far in advance of its time in comparison with virtually all the contemporary European codes. *Russkaia Pravda* prescribed no death penalty, and its provisions were practically free from the cruel punishments so notorious in the penology of the European countries. Almost all the penalties prescribed in the *Pravda* consisted of monetary fines. Somewhat similar provisions were established in other principalities. In general, during the pre-Tatar period Kiev and the other leading principalities and republics of Russia were as advanced in all respects as virtually any European country of the period.

The Tatar invasion and subjugation led to a profound change, especially toward the close of the Tatar domination (which lasted approximately two hundred and fifty years), in connection with the struggle of Muscovy for freedom from this domination. The task of the liberation initiated under the leadership of Muscovy was gigantic, almost hopeless. To carry it through successfully, rigid centralization of the Moscow government and autocratic control by it were absolutely necessary: any war requires a completely centralized and autocratic military power — a hierarchy headed by the commander in chief and embracing every citizen and soldier. Just as in all the democratic countries the present war produced a notable centralization of governmental power, an enormous increase of bureaucratic regimentation, regulation, and control, so the long and desperate struggle of Russia for liberation from the Tatar yoke and for the defense of its national existence against the sinister attacks of many other Asiatic peoples, as well as of such European peoples as the Poles, Swedes, and Teutons, inevitably led to a centralized autocracy so far as the external form of its political regime was concerned. Beginning approximately with John III, this process reached its culmination with the close of the eighteenth century.

However, in order to view the phenomenon in its true perspective, one should bear in mind two cardinal facts. First, even in this period the absolutism of Russian Czarism was far from being complete, all the essential elements of representative government continuing to exist. Second, Russia was no exception to the general rule; for during the centuries in question a like process was under way in practically all the European countries. From the fourteenth century up to the eve of the French Revolution a similar autocratization of the national government — frequently much more drastic — occurred throughout the length and breadth of Europe, reaching its climax in most countries during the sixteenth, seventeenth, and eighteenth centuries. Whereas Russia, in its struggle for liberation, had a genuine excuse for such a transformation, most of the European nations had no such excuse: they were not enslaved or even menaced by the Tatars or other Asiatics, whose fell blows were largely absorbed by Russia itself. Moreover, even during the Muscovy period the autocracy of the Czar was by no means absolute. *The Czar's power was never arbitrary, being constantly defined and limited by law.* The codification of the law in 1550 was followed in 1649 by the enactment of a complete code known as the *Ulojenie* of Czar Alexis Mikhailovitch. This instrument was as comprehensive and advanced as any European code then existing. Furthermore, the authority of the Czar was restricted not only by law but in another way, much more efficient and democratic in character. All the important decrees and governmental decisions of the Muscovy Czar had to be approved by two representative bodies: the *Zemsky Sobor* and the *Boyarskaia Duma*. The *Zemsky Sobor* was a general assembly of the representatives of the principal free classes, very similar in character to the English Parliament and, in particular, to the French *États Généraux*. It was convoked fairly regularly, at frequent intervals, and played in many respects a decisive role. The *Boyarskaia Duma* was a sort of privy council composed of the representatives of the leading aristocratic families of the *boiars*, and resembled the privy councils of Europe. As a contemporary observer, Kotoshikhin, writes: "Although the Czar declared himself an autocrat, he could do nothing without the council of the *boiars*" (the *Boyarskaia Duma*). This council was a permanent body, functioning not intermittently, as did the popular *Sobor*, but regularly.

Thus the Muscovy Czarist regime was as democratic as virtually any contemporary European monarchical regime. The ruler had to decide all political questions with the advice of the *Sobor* or the privy council (the *Duma*), or both. In the *Sobor* and *Duma* the old Russian democratic institution of the *vetsche* was continued, though on a much reduced scale.

Upon the accession of Peter the Great these institutions were unfortunately abolished, being supplanted by a relatively unlimited "enlightened absolutism" similar to that of Frederick the Great, Louis XIV, and other European monarchs. Here, as in many other cases, the imitation of European patterns proved of doubtful benefit to Russia, often leading to the abolition of venerable indigenous institutions superior to those imported to replace them. However, even during the seventeenth and eighteenth centuries certain checks upon the arbitrariness of the Czar continued to exist: namely, the law codes, the Senate, and, later on, the assemblies of the nobility. The only real difference between Russia and some of the most "democratic" European countries was that the explicit replacement of the formally autocratic monarchy by a constitutional monarchy occurred in Russia several decades later than in England, France, Germany, and Austria. After the adoption of the constitution of 1906 Russia became, legally as well as in fact, a constitutional monarchy — more truly constitutional than, for instance, Germany or Austria. In 1917 the monarchy was abolished, being succeeded by a federation of republics.

The foregoing sketch demonstrates the utter fallacy of regarding the so-called autocracy of the Czars as something unique, devoid of any democratic or representative elements. Taken as a whole, the Russian political system from the ninth to the twentieth century was virtually as democratic as the governmental regime of most European nations. Its characterization as an Oriental despotism is accordingly mythical. Moreover, the principal changes which it underwent, in spite of the Tatar domination and the desperateness of Russia's national struggle for existence, were closely paralleled throughout those centuries by the changes to which other Western governmental systems were subjected. Furthermore, the direct influence exerted by Europe in certain periods, for example, during the reign of Peter the Great and those of his successors, operated actually to weaken Muscovy's representative institutions and to re-enforce the Czarist autocracy. This is especially true as regards German influence: the domination of the Kurland-Holstein-Coburg-Brunswick clique, which imitated Frederick the Great's autocracy, represents practically the cruelest, the most autocratic and despotic, and the most sterile chapter in the entire history of the Russian state.

In conclusion, it may be confidently asserted that, contrary to current foreign opinion, Russia's fundamental social structure has always been fully as democratic as that of the European countries. In respect to several of its institutions Russia has, indeed, been more democratic than most of the countries of the West. Even the prerevolutionary *central* government was very similar to that of the European nations. Finally, a comparison of the basic social institutions of Russia and the United States reveals the fact that their points of similarity have been more numerous and significant than their dissimilarities, and that consequently the two nations have been and are, on the whole, essentially congenial.

CHAPTER FIVE

RUSSIAN RELIGIOUS AND ECCLESIASTICAL INSTITUTIONS

1. *The Russian Orthodox Church and Other Religions*

The prevalent conception entertained abroad (especially since the Revolution) concerning the Russian Orthodox Church, and the clergy and religion in general, like many other ideas about the country, has been not only grossly inaccurate but positively grotesque. Fostered by Communist propaganda designed to justify the militant atheism of the Communist rulers and their cruel persecution of Christianity and other faiths during the destructive period of the Revolution, these ideas picture the Russian Orthodox religion as a primitive potpourri compounded of ignorance, prejudice, and superstition, decked out in Oriental ritualism; the clergy as a mongrel breed of magicians, witch doctors, prestidigitators, and exploiters; and the cultural role of the church as that of an "opiate of the people's mind" whose primary social function was to assist the autocratic Czarist regime to exploit the masses and keep them in subjection. In addition, it is claimed that the Orthodox Church, in cooperation with the government, ruthlessly suppressed all other religions. Imbued with such notions, large circles outside Russia, including even part of the Christian clergy, have felt that the Communist antireligious policy was not without justification.

It is hardly necessary to point out the fallacy underlying such opinions. The actual character and the sociocultural role of the Russian Orthodox Church, as well as the true position of other faiths (both Christian and non-Christian) in Russia, may be summarized as follows.

1. Owing to the rather intimate contacts of the Slavic tribes with Byzantium and Bulgaria, Christianity began to penetrate Russia as early as the ninth and tenth centuries.

2. In the tenth century its influence became so strong that in 988 the governmental officials, the army, and the aristocracy of the principality of Kiev accepted Christianity; and presently the rank and file of the population of Kiev and other principalities were likewise converted (partly, to be sure, through coercion). In due course it became the official, or state religion. This step, however, was not taken hastily or in haphazard fashion, but only after a fairly long investigation and comparison of the relative merits of the Jewish, Mohammedan, and "Latin" religions. First their representatives were invited by Prince Vladimir to his court, where they pleaded the case of their respective faiths; whereupon a delegation of "wise men" was sent to Byzantium and other centers to investigate these systems at first hand. Only after a thoroughgoing examination of each of them was the Byzantine-Bulgarian form of Christianity finally adopted.

3. The Greek form of Christianity was at that time not yet sharply differentiated either theologically or formally from the "Latin" form, whose seat was at Rome. Dogmatic differences were then of secondary importance, the principal issues being psychosocial factors and rivalry for administrative supremacy. Constantinople, or Byzantium, was at that time the chief heir of Greco-Roman culture; one of the foremost centers of Christianity in the world; the seat of virtually the most powerful empire in Christendom; and the most magnificent city in the entire West, far surpassing Rome in the fields of fine arts, science, philosophy, law, and so forth. Moreover, the Byzantine religion had emerged from the "Iconoclastic" struggle as a sound and virile faith. In view of all these circumstances Russia's choice was both comprehensible

and sensible from many standpoints. It gave pagan Russia a fully developed form of Christianity. It introduced well-educated Greek priests, missionaries, etc. who constituted Russia's first religious teachers and clergy. Byzantium supplied, moreover, the artists, architects, and other craftsmen essential for the erection and decoration of churches and the building of ecclesiastical schools, hospitals, orphanages, almshouses, and similar institutions. Again, Byzantium furnished learned scribes who translated or transcribed the most important existing religious books, including the *Scriptures* and the *Nomokanon,* or Byzantine code of canon law.

4. Owing to the rapid diffusion of Byzantine Christianity (which was destined to be gradually Russianized, by imperceptible degrees), it became almost immediately one of the basic forces in the historical development of the Russian government, society, and culture and an integral part of the psychology of the Russian people, which can, indeed, hardly be conceived of apart from its influence. The power of the newly adopted Christian religion is typically illustrated by the striking transformation which it wrought in the personality of Prince (or "Saint") Vladimir, who introduced it, and in that of his immediate successors. Extremely sensual, violent, and belligerent by nature, after his conversion he became so gentle that, heeding the Biblical injunction "Thou shalt not kill," he hesitated to punish even criminals. In the spirit of Christian charity he ordered that his palace should be kept open at all times for the poor and unfortunate, who were to be fed and cared for, and that those who could not come to the palace should be provided with food and other necessities. He undertook likewise the building of churches, orphan asylums, ecclesiastical schools, and so on. The notable law code *Russian Truth* (*Russkaia Pravda*), enacted by his successor Prince Jaroslav the Wise (1016-1054), abolished capital punishment and torture for all crimes, replacing these penalties with monetary fines. The next distinguished prince, Vladimir

Monomach (1113-1125), both in his way of life and in his "Testament" bequeathed to his successors, reveals the profound metamorphosis of a pagan Norse warrior, who derided Christianity as something suited only to weak women, into a meek and lowly follower of the Nazarene. "Have the fear of God in your hearts and perform incessantly the work of charity — this is the foundation of everything good." "Don't forswear your oath." "Do not permit the strong to harm the weak." "Do not kill either the innocent or the guilty, not even if the guilty deserve the death penalty." "When you and your troops are traveling through the Russian lands, do not allow your guard or your retinue to exploit and oppress the population; wherever you stop, give food and drink to all who ask for them." "Get up early, before the sunrise; pray to God; and then sit down with your companions to deliberate on the state affairs and to render justice." One can hardly imagine a greater contrast to the pre-Christian pagan warrior!

Early Russian Christianity expressed itself not only in preaching and divine service but in a fundamental reshaping of the character of the people, their institutions, and their culture. It was responsible for the establishment of Russia's first schools; it produced the first law codes; it introduced courts for the judgment of the clergy as well as of the people in ethical and religious matters; it improved family life and raised the general standard of morality; it fostered charitable institutions and a system of social service; it opposed and ameliorated the harsh forms of slavery and serfdom; it shaped the hierarchical principle of social stratification and differentiation; it translated and circulated the first books; it initiated the fine arts — literature and the drama, painting, architecture, and music; and it laid the foundations of Russian philosophy and *Weltanschauung*. In a word, its religious, ethical, social, and cultural impact was overwhelming.

5. Throughout the entire subsequent history of Russia, the Christian Church has served the people in both their joys

and their sorrows. Its role has been particularly salutary and helpful in the tragic crises when the independence or the very existence of the nation has been at stake, as during the Tatar invasions; the incursions of Turks, Poles, Swedes, and Teutons; the assaults of Napoleon and Hitler's legions; and the grave periods of internal anarchy, such as the "Times of Trouble" at the beginning of the seventeenth century. Without the ministrations of the church it is doubtful whether Russia could have managed to survive certain of these crises.

In view of the manifold and vital functions performed by the Russian Orthodox religion, it has probably played a more important role than any branch of the Christian Church in most of the European countries. As I have said, it has been well-nigh completely identified with the Russian nation. In its absence the structure of Russian society and culture would have been as inchoate and incomprehensible as that of medieval Europe without Roman Catholicism. Hence the absurdity of the conception of the Russian ecclesiastical system as a burden artificially imposed upon the people.

This identification of the state religion with the national soul explains, moreover, the exclusive value attached to it in Russia's social and cultural life up to the Revolution, as well as the gradually increasing value assigned it since the close of the destructive phase of the Revolution. We have seen that Russia has hardly known the principle of racial, or ethnic, discrimination. If certain groups such as the Jews or Poles or pagans have been discriminated against, this has been due not to their race or nationality but to their *religion*; and as soon as they have accepted Russian Orthodox Christianity, all limitations upon their rights and privileges have automatically ceased.

This accounts also for the somewhat privileged position allotted to the Russian Orthodox religion (in contradistinction especially to non-christian sects) before the beginning of the twentieth century. However, this privileged position did not entail the suppression of other faiths in prerevolutionary Russia, or even their persecution. As a matter of fact, it did not differ sharply from the pre-eminence, for instance, of the Anglican Church among the various other religious denominations of England; and it was certainly less striking than, let us say, the exclusive sway exercised by the dominant church faction in colonial Massachusetts. All the Christian denominations, as well as Judaism, Mohammedanism, and many pagan religions, were tolerated and openly carried on their respective activities. Moreover, it was the state which actually paid the greater part of the salaries of the Roman Catholic and Protestant clergy. The only sects that were prohibited were those regarded as antisocial, such as the Khlysti, whose revivals were attended by sexual orgies, or the Skoptzi, whose practices involved the mutilation of the genitals. It was but natural that the government should have encouraged conversion to the Orthodox faith and, per contra, should have frowned upon the adherence of former members of the state church to other religions. But in so far as conversion to other religions was hindered by legal methods, it was inhibited only indirectly, in the sense that a convert forfeited certain of the privileges he had enjoyed as a member of the Orthodox Church. Such discriminations as existed (for the most part de facto rather than legal) were eventually abolished by the constitution and reforms of 1906 and the following years.

Finally, the record of the Russian state church is far freer from the guilt of large-scale religious wars and persecutions than that of the Roman Catholic Church and even of some of the Protestant denominations (notably the Calvinists). In its treatment of "heretics" and unbelievers it exhibits nothing comparable to the cruelty of the Inquisition (from the twelfth to the sixteenth century), the ruthless wars against the Albigensians and Huguenots, or the massacre of St. Bartholomew.

Apart from the coercive measures employed by the Kiev

Government after its adoption of Christianity, virtually the sole historical example of serious religious dissension relates to the sharp clash between two *rival factions within the Russian Church* — namely, the so-called "Old Believers" and the "Nikonians," during the reign of Czar Alexei Mikhailovitch (1645-1676). The reforms carried out by the Patriarch Nikon — concerning such matters as the correct text of the *Scriptures,* the proper spelling of the name of Jesus, the representation of the Cross with four or eight arms, the increase in the authority of the Patriarch at the expense of that of the Czar, and so forth — encountered stubborn resistance. This opposition led in several instances to persecution of the "Old Believers" at the hands of the state. Some were imprisoned, others banished; and the public observance of their faith was prohibited. Some of the recalcitrants went so far as to invite martyrdom by deliberately burning themselves alive in the ruins of their churches doomed to be closed or demolished by the government. But, despite its acuteness, this clash was merely an *internal* dispute — not a struggle between Russian and non-Russian forms of Christianity.

2. *Theological and Philosophical Aspects of the Russian Orthodox Religion*

Taken in its theological, philosophical, moral, and social aspects, the Russian Orthodox religion differs from Roman Catholicism and Protestantism in many ways; but none of these differences affords a proper basis for regarding the Russian type of Christianity as inferior to any of the other important Christian denominations.

Theologically and ritually it is very similar to the "High Church" wing of the Protestant Episcopal Church; the two are, indeed, so closely akin that their respective services can readily be interchanged. Theologically, the main difference between Eastern Christianity (including the Russian religion) and Roman Catholicism relates to the famous term *filioque* in the Roman Catholic Credo — that is, the question whether the Holy Ghost emanates from God the Father only, as the Eastern Church contends, or from God the Son also (*filioque*), as is held by the Roman Catholic Church. This difference, as is well known, was the principal bone of contention responsible for the regrettable final cleavage of Christianity (in 1054) into its Eastern and Western branches.

In its spirit and philosophy the Russian Orthodox Church occupies an intermediate position between Roman Catholicism and Protestantism. It is, of course, very difficult to give in a few words an authentic picture of the "soul" of any great religion. But the essential differences between the "souls" of the three foremost branches of Christianity, *as they have appeared to most eminent Russian theologians, religious thinkers, and philosophers,* such as V. Soloviev and F. M. Dostoevski, may be summed up as follows. The Russian religion is less dogmatic and authoritarian than Roman Catholicism, but more so than Protestantism. The hierarchical principle in the Russian Church is more fully developed than in most of the Protestant denominations, but less so than in the Church of Rome. The Russian Patriarch has never possessed as much authority as the Pope; and he has never claimed either supremacy over the other patriarchs or infallibility, as does the Pope. The Russian Patriarch has been simply *primus inter pares* among the high prelates of the Russian Church. To eminent Russian thinkers like Dostoevski, Roman Catholicism, as a religio-political system, appeared, as a marvelous mechanism that had forfeited, to a large extent, the vital spirit of Jesus. Protestantism, per contra, impressed them as essentially a protest against Catholicism — a negative phenomenon that could neither thrive nor even continue to exist in the absence of the object of its protest. In his "Three Ideas" and in the "Legend of the Great Inquisitor" in his *Brothers Karamazov,*

Dostoevski develops a striking picture of the Roman Catholic, Protestant, and Russian churches. According to his conception and that of other leading Russian religious and philosophical thinkers, the Russian Church occupies a middle position: it is much less of a mechanism than the Church of Rome, and much less deeply imbued with a spirit of protest than the Protestant denominations. Similarly, it is less formal than the Catholic system and more formal than Protestantism. It gives wider latitude to human reason, experience, and intuition in religion and ethics than Catholicism, but less than many Protestant denominations. It does not require unconditional and unquestioning acceptance of the dicta of the church authorities, such as Roman Catholicism insists on, thus permitting a much larger margin of autonomy for the searching mind of the believer; neither does it leave the whole matter to the reason or inspiration of the individual, as do certain Protestant denominations. It is more intimate and warm-hearted, less coldly rational and authoritarian, than Catholicism, but less "anarchic" and "spontaneously revivalistic" than Protestantism. It strongly stresses the free, spontaneous, all-embracing love of God to man and of man to God, rather than unquestioning obedience to the dicta of authority, as in Roman Catholicism and Calvinism, or the utilitarian freedom characteristic of most Protestant sects.

According to Dostoevski, Catholicism made three primary forces the very foundation of its teaching and existence — namely, authority, mystery (or dogma), and miracles. His Great Inquisitor reproaches Jesus for rejecting these forces when he was tempted by the Great Tempter in the Wilderness. For the sake of the happiness of mankind, declares the Inquisitor, we accepted all of them. "Eight centuries ago we accepted from the Great Tempter what Thou didst indignantly reject. We took from him Rome and the sword of Caesar and declared ourselves the sole earthly emperors. . . . Although this undertaking is still far from being fully accomplished, and mankind is destined meanwhile to undergo great suffering, we shall ultimately achieve it, becoming the world's Caesars, and we shall then be in a position to realize the happiness of all mankind."

Likewise, the Inquisitor continues, we accepted from the Great Tempter authoritarian secret dogma, which should be obeyed blindly by all men because it is absolutely essential to their happiness, and is in this sense highly utilitarian. The same is true of the utilitarian "miracle" of changing stones into bread, which Jesus refused to perform when the Great Tempter besought him to do so. "Thou didst not realize that if man rejects miracles, he will also reject God, because man looks not so much for God as for miracles . . . Thou didst not descend from the cross when they insultingly shouted, 'Descend from the cross, and we will then believe that Thou art the Son of God.' Thou didst not descend because Thou didst not wish to enslave man by means of miracles, desiring free and spontaneous faith — not miraculous faith. [In refusing to transform stones into bread, as the Great Tempter desired] Thou didst not want to deprive man of his freedom; for Thou didst think that there could be no freedom if obedience and faith were bought by bread. Thou saidest that man cannot live by bread alone."

By means of these and like *exaggerations*, Dostoevski and other notable Russian religious thinkers bring out several significant differences between the Russian, Roman Catholic, and Protestant types of "religious soul." The principle of Caesarism has certainly found far less authentic expression in the Russian ecclesiastical system than in Roman Catholicism or Calvinism. The same is true of the principle of blind obedience to dogma or that of empirical utilitarianism in the field of religion.

In its spirit and philosophy the Russian Orthodox Church is much closer to the Eastern Church Fathers, such as Gregory of Nyssa, Saint Basil, Pseudo-Dionysius, and Saint John

Chrysostom, than to Saint Augustine; and it finds among Western religious thinkers a closer affinity to Johannus Scotus Erigena and Saint Francis of Assisi than to Saint Thomas Aquinas or Calvin, or to Pope Leo the Great, Pope Gregory IX, and similar distinguished organizers of the Church of Rome. Its spirit of mysticism has been as strong as that of Roman Catholicism, and even stronger than that of Protestantism; but this spirit has exhibited more informal and hence more diverse and unorthodox patterns than that of Western Catholicism.

These points of divergence between the Russian religion and other types of Christianity suffice to show that the former is in no sense more primitive, superstitious, or obscurantist than the latter. The intermediate position which the "soul" of the Russian religion occupies between the polar "souls" of Roman Catholicism and Protestantism in itself argues against such an assumption. Avoiding the two extremes, it has impressed many thoughtful minds as being more balanced and harmonious than either Roman Catholicism or Protestantism. When one studies both its past and its comparatively recent theological and philosophical works, one is forced to admit that in their own way they are as profound as the foremost contributions of Roman Catholic and Protestant theological and philosophical thought. Among recent works those of Skovoroda, Vladimir Soloviev, Dostoevski, Florenski (in his *Pillar and Affirmation of Truth*), N. Losski, and N. Berdiaiev give a fairly adequate idea of the spirit and philosophy of the Russian religion.

3. *Hierarchical Organization*

Hierarchically the Russian Church was originally subordinated to the Byzantine Church, being under the jurisdiction of its Patriarch. In a comparatively short time, however, it became actually and then legally independent of this jurisdiction. The Russian Patriarch, *elected* by the authorized representatives of the Russian religion, became its head (1588). At no time in its history was it subject to the control of the Roman Catholic See.

The administrative and guiding role of the Russian Patriarch was a powerful one, and most of the patriarchs discharged their duties faithfully and to good effect. Especially noteworthy were the services rendered to Russia by its patriarchs and other religious leaders during periods of acute crisis. Whether in the consolidation of Russia into a single nation, or in coping with internal crises, or in seeking to save the country from foreign conquest (such as the Tatar yoke), the religious leaders of Russia played as valiant a part as her foremost princes, czars, and other secular leaders. Such names as those of Abbotts, Theodosy Petcherski, Sergius Radonejski, Abram Palytzyn, Dionysius, and the patriarchs Hermogen, Peter, Alexis, Jona, and Philipp, are stamped indelibly upon the pages of Russian history. The pre-Patriarchal and Patriarchal epochs were, on the whole, heroic, creative, and democratic. Directly and indirectly the church was a genuine *Corpus Mysticum*. Its leaders and clerical personnel were recruited from all classes of the population. The hierarchy was democratic in spirit, closely united with the people, and largely elective — a true *sobor,* or religious collective entity. From all these standpoints it was no less democratic and no more autocratic (if the terms can properly be applied to religion and the church) than the other Christian religions of the West.

Unfortunately, the reforms of Peter the Great terminated the Patriarchy (in 1721) and considerably curtailed the independence and the creative role of the church. Like other "enlightened monarchical reformers," he sought to eliminate all rivalry between the church and the state, and all efforts to block the reforms initiated by the government — in a word, to destroy all independence of church policy. Hence he abolished the Patriarchy, replacing it with a collective *Synod,* an ecclesiastical college composed of metropolitans and bishops, as the supreme church authority, and appointing a High Procurator as his personal representative for the supervision of the Synod and the co-ordination of the Synod's policies with those of the government. The objective results of these ill-advised reforms were, among others, a certain loss of independence in connection with the judicial, social, and economic functions of the church; the bureaucratization of its administrative apparatus; the subordination of the hierarchy to the Czarist Government; a decrease in the spontaneous collectivity of the church (at least in the upper strata of the hierarchy); and the replacement of democratic principles by autocratic ones in the selection of the hierarchs and other leaders and in ecclesiastical functions in general. The vital creative unity of the church in its upper ranks was supplanted by the official machinery so vigorously denounced by Dostoevski.

However, one should not exaggerate these defects, as has recently been done by Communists and other detractors of the Russian ecclesiastical system. For while Peter's reforms radically changed the administrative mechanism in the upper strata, they did not fundamentally alter the basic character of the Russian religion; the religious aspirations, attitudes, and beliefs of the people; or the functions of the rank and file of the clergy. These continued to function essentially as they had done before. The church continued to stand by the people, particularly throughout the darkest periods of Russian history, such as those of the domination of the state by German cliques, the Napoleonic invasion, and the like. Similarly the people stood by the church. Peter's reforms accordingly failed to sever the ties binding the nation and the church into a single unity.

4. The Decline of Religion Before the Revolution

If notable changes occurred in the period from 1721 to 1917, they were due not so much to the aforesaid reforms as to the general change of sociocultural conditions in Russia and to the altered mentality of some of the Russian classes. This change in the "cultural climate" led to a decrease of religious-mindedness on the part of the educated classes; a notable decline of the prestige of the church among certain sections of the population; a weakening of the spiritual leadership of the church; a slackening and bureaucratization of religious functions in the case of some of the priests and prelates; and a general decline in the creative role of the church. The "subserviency of the Russian Church to Czardom" was by no means as widespread and serious as its calumniators have claimed. As has been said, the decline in question was due to much more fundamental causes — namely, to a profound transformation of the culture and mentality of Russian society akin to that experienced by European society. This conclusion is supported by the fact that a similar decline was experienced by other branches of Christianity throughout the West: the prestige and decisive role of medieval Christianity decreased there also from the fourteenth century on.

Especially acute was the decline of religious feeling among the educated classes. The more revolutionary element became open disbelievers and outright atheists, equally inimical to Christianity and to non-Christian faiths. Another element lost its erstwhile religious fervor; still another continued to adhere to the church, but only in routine fashion. A similar spirit of irreligiousness — marked by greater vulgarity — invaded other classes, notably the urban population. Though the bulk of the peasantry remained outwardly religious, nevertheless their piety became more and more a ritualistic affair — a matter of ceremonies, prayers, services, and other standardized, formalized activities. The living spirit of religion was everywhere withering. During the second half of the nineteenth century this process gained added momentum, continuing up to 1917. Hence it will be seen that the anti-religious trend was not initiated by the Revolution but existed long before it.

5. *The Reformation of the Church and Its Persecution During the Revolution*

One of the first acts of the Revolution was the proclamation by the Provisional Government (headed by Prince Lvov and then by Kerenski) of complete freedom of religion. Simultaneously the church and the nation seized the opportunity to divest the church of its subservience to the government, first introduced by the reform of Peter the Great; to separate it from the state; to re-establish the Patriarchy in place of the bureaucratic Synod; to eliminate all the undesirable traits that it had acquired; and to restore the heroic and truly creative role it had played before the reforms of Peter the Great. In the summer of 1917 an all-Russian *Sobor* (or Congress) of the duly elected representatives of all the faithful was held in Moscow and unanimously voted these and many other reforms. The Metropolitan Tikhon, a former representative of the Russian Church in the United States, was elected as Patriarch. The revival of religion and the church began to proceed apace. If the church had only been granted a few years for the consummation of this promising renaissance, there is hardly any doubt that a new creative and heroic religious epoch would have been ushered in.

Unfortunately, the Communist Revolution attempted by every means to destroy religion in general and the Russian Orthodox system in particular. Its murderous attacks were launched precisely at a time when the Russian Church had become as free and democratic as possible. While hypocritically declaring for freedom of religion, the Communist Government, in the name of militant atheism, branded all religion as "an opiate of the people's mind" and embarked upon a pitiless and brutal persecution directed particularly against the Orthodox Church. In a volume entitled *The Truth about Religion in Russia,* published officially in 1942 by the Moscow Patriarchy and consisting of a series of articles by high Russian prelates, it is declared that there has been no persecution of religion at the hands of the Soviet Government. Such understatement may be excused on the part of the acting Patriarch, the Moscow Metropolitan Sergius; for though present conditions are far different from those attending the destructive phase of the Revolution, nevertheless the Patriarch and the church in general are still in the power of the Soviet Government, and hence can hardly afford to be frank and sincere. With all due respect for Patriarch Sergius, the facts of the persecution of religion during the first phase of the Revolution are too numerous, too well ascertained, too undeniable, to be annulled by the statement of even the head of the Russian Church. Here are a few of the facts. Most of the church buildings and practically all other ecclesiastical property (including even gold, silver, and valuable ritual objects) were seized by the government, regardless of the protest of the parishioners to whom the church buildings and all their appurtenances belonged. Other churches were compulsorily closed, being converted now into Communist clubs, now into warehouses, and so on. This hardly looks like religious freedom! Moreover, it was forbidden, under fairly severe penalties, to give religious instruction to any group of persons with the exception of instruction in the family, where the number of those receiving such instruction must not exceed five or so. Even this was frowned upon and not infrequently penalized. During the years when the barest means of subsistence could be obtained only through

ration cards, the clergy either were given no cards at all —
and were therefore practically doomed to death by starvation — or were allotted a minimum ration sufficient only to
prevent their "forgetting how bread smells" (the wording of
Zinoviev, then a big Communist boss, later "purged" and
liquidated). This again does not look like freedom of religion.
Furthermore, religious ceremonies could not be performed
outside church buildings. Finally, more than a thousand of
the clergy and religious-minded civilians were summarily
arrested and executed. Hypocritically, the official reason
given for the execution was "counterrevolutionary activities."
But since purely religious functions were regarded (now explicitly, now implicitly) as counterrevolution, and since the
overwhelming majority of the victims had not participated in
any real counterrevolutionary activities, the falsity of the
official subterfuge is all too clear. Several of my colleagues at
the University of Petrograd and several of my friends and
acquaintances were executed merely because of their active
participation in religious activities: they had not the remotest
connection with any real counterrevolutionary work. Exact
statistics of these victims are not available; for during the
destructive period of the Revolution, executions were conducted on such a large scale (at least five hundred thousand
were slain) that nobody bothered to record the number. The
victims of religious persecution who were executed include
at least twenty-eight bishops and twelve hundred and nineteen priests, to say nothing of the thousands of humbler believers. To these may be added the much larger number of
persons imprisoned, sent to concentration camps, or condemned to hard labor (and thus doomed to slow death).

Consider the children and other relatives of religious-
minded persons, particularly those of the clergy who were
discriminated against for "the sins of their fathers." Add to
this the loss of civil and political rights suffered by the faithful. Consider, further, the atheistic propaganda, conducted

by influential Communist leaders and officially sanctioned and financed, with its dozens of journals and magazines, ridiculing, satirizing, and denouncing God, Christ, the Virgin, and all the basic values of religion in the most unrestrained and frequently virulent and indecent terms. Bear in mind that the "militant atheists" did not confine themselves to publications and speeches, but often raided the churches, interrupted the services, and openly perpetrated (from the standpoint of true believers) the most sacrilegious acts. Under the threat of drastic punishment, such propaganda and other activities could not be openly opposed: no counterpropaganda or other resistance was tolerated.

These facts suffice to demonstrate the rigor of the persecution of religion carried out by the Communist regime during the initial phase of the Revolution. In its severity it rivals almost any religious persecution known to history.

Overtaking the church at the moment of its revival and reconstruction, this persecution, together with measures directed to the same end, exerted temporarily a profound influence. The younger generation, virtually deprived of religious instruction (especially in the urban centers), grew up either actively irreligious or at least wholly indifferent to religion. Many an adult, in the face of threatened punishment and the loss of certain privileges, lost much of his religious zeal. The church itself — the clergy as well as the parishioners — split into several factions, including the "New Churchmen" (or *Novo-Zerkovnik*), who became subservient henchmen of the Communist Government, and factions radically opposed to the government (these factions, of course, could openly exist only abroad, among the Russian exiles). The Patriarch Tikhon, as a prisoner of the Communist Government, could exert no unifying power; he was under strict surveillance unable either to move about freely or to publish anything not sanctioned by the Soviet authorities. His voice was thus completely silenced. In 1925 he died. His successor, the acting

Patriarch[1] Bishop Peter, was soon arrested and banished to Siberia. His successor, in turn, Bishop (and then Metropolitan) Sergius, adopted a policy of collaboration, within decent limits, with the Communist regime. Such a policy naturally proved wholly ineffective during the first phase of the Revolution, leading to a loss of prestige of the acting Patriarch among many groups of believers; to the formal repudiation of his authority by a number of the hierarchy, both in Russia and abroad; to the administrative separation of several Russian churches abroad (in Europe generally, and in the United States, Canada, and elsewhere) from the existing Russian Patriarchy; and to similar results.

The unity of the Russian Church was thus finally broken. Its hierarchical structure was split up into a number of factions. For the time being, it had ceased to constitute a single *Corpus Mysticum.*

6. *The Revival of Religion in the Post-Destructive Period of the Revolution*

Every serious investigator of profound revolutions is aware that they destroy only those institutions, values, and trends that were already moribund and would have ultimately perished even in the absence of any revolutionary upheaval. Institutions, values, and trends that are sound, vigorous, and fundamental, although they may be temporarily disrupted during the destructive phase of a revolution, invariably revive, after the passing of this negative phase, in a purified

[1] The Patriarch must be elected by the All-Russian Congress of duly elected representatives of the church — clergy as well as laymen. Under the Soviet regime such a *sobor*, or congress, could not be convoked; and in any case it would have lacked the necessary freedom for the conduct of its deliberations. Hence after the death of Patriarch Tikhon no new Patriarch could be chosen. Instead, an "Acting Patriarch" — or, rather a *substitute* for the Patriarch — was appointed. However in 1943 the Patriarchy was restored and the acting Patriarch was elected as Patriarch.

and ennobled form, resuming their prerevolutionary course and carrying it to its logical conclusion. Their power, indeed, is so irresistible that the revolution is ultimately compelled to recognize and sanction them, even going so far as to pretend that, instead of having sought to oppose them, it has consistently endeavored to preserve and cherish them. As we shall see, this is precisely what has happened with many basic institutions and values during the post-destructive phase of the Russian Revolution. Among them is the Russian religious system.

During the nineteen thirties a gradual, almost imperceptible change became evident in the field of the Russian church and religion and in the policy of the government vis-à-vis these institutions. In the first place, although the number of religious-minded persons had certainly greatly decreased, it was noted that those who had retained their faith, as well as those newly converted from their erstwhile position as atheists, were animated by a religious ardor of singular intensity. Purified and ennobled by the tragedy which their nation had undergone, their religious sense transcended the comparatively low level of routine ritualism and inherited custom and soared to exalted heights, envisaging a union with God and His eternal values unblemished by any mundane motives. As such it became an utterly fearless and irresistible force, taking complete possession of the body and soul of the believer.

This transformation occurred in many different classes. The intelligentsia, hitherto perhaps more atheistic or agnostic than that of any other country, became, for the most part, acutely religious-minded. University professors and representatives of other professions who had scarcely ever delivered a sermon prior to the Revolution now frequently felt impelled to preach to church congregations. Other elements of the educated classes adopted an attitude of sincere respect for religion as one of the foremost cultural forces. The former agnostic or atheistic and hostile attitude toward religion largely disappeared. The cases of S. Bulgakov and N. Berdiaiev, professors of political economy at the University of Moscow, are typical. They were among the few intellectuals who constituted the first notable Russian Marxians and introduced Marxism into Russia. During the Revolution, Bulgakov was ordained as a priest and became the head of the Russian Theological Institute in Paris; and Berdiaiev became an eminent religious thinker and philosopher. The addresses of the writer before large audiences of professors and students at Petrograd in 1921 and 1922, on the anniversary of the founding of the university — addresses in which the role of religion was highly extolled — were received with thunderous applause which drowned out the protests of the Communists — something which would have been quite impossible before the Revolution. A similar religious transformation manifested itself among the peasantry and other classes, including even a section of the Communist party itself. An impartial observer who attended the church services during these years, if he had been familiar with the atmosphere prevalent before the Revolution, would have been amazed by the intensity of the religious fervor displayed by the congregation. A sensitive observer could not have failed to detect an atmosphere akin to that which probably prevailed in the early Christian catacombs — a spirit of unbounded religious aspiration, devotion, and faith in God, and of willingness, if necessary, to die for one's faith.

In some this metamorphosis assumed the form of mysticism and gnosticism, in the truest sense of the terms. In the majority of cases it assumed the guise of devotion to the Russian Orthodox religion in a purified and highly spiritualized form. Some of the latter adhered to the ritual and other traditional ceremonials, regularly attending the church services and submitting to the administrative guidance of the Moscow Patriarchy, its acting head, and the other ecclesiastical authorities. Others, more concerned with inner, subjective values, regarded the ritual as something secondary — as a means rather than an end — and hence tended somewhat to ignore the externals of the Orthodox faith. These distinctions are made in order to emphasize the fact that *the magnitude of the religious revival in question cannot be properly apprehended solely on the basis of attendance upon church services and of the official records of the number of believers.*

A similar renaissance made itself felt within the ranks of the priesthood and the hierarchy. The weaker personalities — those who were earning their livelihood as officials of the Church Department, who attached greater importance to Mammon than to God, or who were afraid of incurring disfranchisement and like penalties — all these were gradually weeded out during the fiery ordeal of the Revolution. Preferring to play safe by courting the favor of the ruling class, they forswore the priesthood and became "seculars," loyally subservient to the Communist authorities. Only those who were true servants of God, putting their spiritual duties above all other considerations, remained within the ranks of the clergy. Purified and transfigured by the tragic ordeal through which they and their country had passed, they have measured up to the most exalted standards of religious and ethical leadership, and have thus gained added authority and prestige in the eyes of all the faithful whom they so devotedly and wholeheartedly serve.

Revitalized both within the ranks of the clergy and in the hearts of the people, religion naturally began to exert (through intangible and subtle means) an ever-increasing influence upon the nation and the government. Firmly entrenched in power, and with the church relegated exclusively to religious in distinction from political functions, the government eventually lost its hysterical paranoiac disposition to detect on every hand evidences of sinister "counterrevolutionary" activities. This led to an abatement of its policy of persecution. Faced with the paramount task of social reconstruction, it came to perceive the need for actual co-operation with the church. Coercive police measures, so effective for purposes of suppression, were discovered to be wholly inadequate — if not actually impotent — as a means of rebuilding the family; of educating the masses; of inculcating honesty, social-mindedness, and altruism; of developing the arts and sciences, economics, and politics. Finally, when the imminence of war became apparent, and it was necessary to arouse a popular sense of loyalty, heroic courage, and readiness for supreme sacrifice, the co-operation of the forces of religion became even more imperative. Although not many were prepared to fight and die for either Stalin or the Communist party, the rank and file were willing, as always, to sacrifice themselves for the *fatherland* and its basic historical values. Among these fundamental values were religion and the church. As in previous crises, these institutions could be counted on to inculcate a spirit of loyalty, courage, and sacrifice.

Under such circumstances the religious policy of the government was bound to be progressively transformed, manifesting first an attitude of increasing tolerance and then an open recognition of the positive values of religion, including lavish praise for the services of such leaders as Prince ("Saint") Alexander Nevski and the various patriarchs, bishops, abbots, and priests who had helped to create Russia, and to organize resistance to the enemy in the darkest hours of foreign invasion.

This shift of policy reacted, in turn, upon the religious renaissance itself. With the decline of the Communist persecution, many who had been cowed by repression began to return to the fold of the church. Many religious customs, including the observance of Christmas and Easter, were restored; Sunday and holy days were increasingly observed; and church attendance rapidly mounted, even among members of the Communist party. Atheistic propaganda abated and soon almost reached the vanishing point. At present its organizations are virtually disbanded, its publications have largely ceased to function, and it no longer derives any appreciable funds from the government treasury.

The invasion of the country by Hitler's legions gave an enormous impetus to this religious revival. Contrary to his expectations, the Nazi attack served merely to weld Russians of all factions and creeds into an indivisible unity — a single entity unconditionally resolved to fight for Russia's freedom and independence. No sooner was the first assault launched than the church and its leaders called upon the citizenry to rally to the support of the fatherland. To this challenge the faithful responded without stint, contributing money and valuables, food, clothing, and almost anything they possessed to the defense of the country. Parishioners and priests alike joined the armed forces, loyally co-operating with the government. The latter, in its turn, naturally evinced a progressively friendly attitude toward the church, whose services it so urgently required. At the present it sanctioned the restoration of the Patriarchy, enlarged religious freedom, and ceased religious persecution.

It would, of course, be incorrect to assume that the trend in question has already reached its culmination. The covert attitude of the Soviet authorities toward religion is probably still one of hostility, suspicion, or, at least, indifference. Nevertheless, a minimum of religious freedom has been achieved; and this will undoubtedly steadily increase, regardless of the ideology of the political regime. Meanwhile the government itself, impelled by the pressure of powerful historical forces, will inevitably assume an attitude of growing friendliness toward the co-operation with the various religious organizations of the nation.

To summarize: after the long prerevolutionary period of gradual decline, followed by the tragic disintegration incident in the first phase of the Revolution, the Russian religious system rapidly began to revive, purified, sublimated, ennobled, and revitalized by the fiery ordeal of the crisis through which it had passed. It is now potentially as strong as that of any country — probably stronger than in many — possessing immense latent resources of faith and moral power. Its present strategic situation and internal constitution are such as to preclude any apprehension as to the future status of religion in Russia, pointing, indeed, to a spiritual renaissance as notable as any in the annals of Russian ecclesiastical history.

In conclusion it may be said that, all in all, the Russian religion and church throughout the centuries have been virtually as democratic as any comparable religious system in the world. At the present time they are intimately identified with the spiritual, ethical, and psychological needs of the masses. Moreover, they are *free* — exempt from control by the state and shorn of the last vestiges of the dead weight of bureaucracy.

CHAPTER SIX

THE MORAL STANDARDS OF THE TWO NATIONS

1. *Russia*

"Scratch a Russian and you will find a Tatar!" This familiar saying means that, ethically and socially, the Russians are barbarians, for whom no moral norms are sacred, no human or divine laws inviolate. Being merely wild Scythians, they are believed to be a grave menace to civilization, culture, and morality. Variations upon this theme have been repeated *ad infinitum et ad nauseam* by self-appointed crusaders and saviors of civilization, including Adolf Hitler and his "minister of enlightenment," Herr Goebbels.

We have seen in the preceding chapters that politically, socially, psychologically, and religiously the characteristics of the Russian nation in no way conform to such a picture. If we take an absolute standard of morality, such as the Sermon on the Mount, we must conclude that *all nations*, without exception, are barbarians. Thus far, the Christian ideals embodied in the Sermon on the Mount have been fully realized by only a few saintly *individuals*. If we apply a *relative* standard of morality and sociality, we find that Russia is as sound as any other nation.

In the interest of the maximum clarity, let us take *one of the most reliable practical barometers of social morality — namely, criminality*. Such statistics, needless to say, are defective in all countries; but they nevertheless furnish an approximately accurate gauge. Whether one considers the statistics of crimes against persons (murder, manslaughter, assault and battery, rape and other sex crimes) or those against property (theft, larceny, robbery, forgery, etc.), or the records of offenses against public decency; whether one takes the frequency of crime per one thousand of the total population, the adult population, the occupational population, or the urban and rural population; or whether one measures criminality by the data of arrests, imprisonments, and convictions — in all these respects *the relative index of criminality in Russia during normal periods* (that is, exclusive of periods of revolution) *will be found to be one of the lowest in comparison with that of the European countries.*[1] In so far as the graver forms of criminality are symptomatic of acute immorality and anti-social conduct, Russia stands near the top of the social scale. This conclusion is the more convincing in that the penal system prior to the Revolution was extremely mild. As has been said, the penal code abolished capital punishment as early as about the middle of the eighteenth century for all crimes except attempts against the life of the Czar and his family.

The principal reasons for the phenomenon in question are not far to seek. Urban and industrial centers exhibit, as a rule, a higher crime ratio than the rural population. The agricultural class generally presents a lower degree of criminality than the other occupational classes with the exception of the professions and a few others. Moreover, well-defined mores make for greater ethical stability than loose and rapidly shifting mores. Since Russia, prior to the twentieth century, was more agricultural, less urbanized and industrialized, than the majority of the Western countries, this factor in itself is sufficient to account for its relatively low rate of criminality, as in the case of the predominantly agricultural Balkan countries.

The Revolution of 1905-1906 and especially that of 1917 and the subsequent years resulted in a sharp upswing in the crime rate. But in *every* country the social instability asso-

---

[1] The index of criminality in Russia has been distinctly lower than, for instance, that of Germany. Hence the arrant hypocrisy of the slogans of the Hitlerite "crusaders."

ciated with major internal convulsions invariably leads to heightened criminality. In this respect Russia's record merely conforms to the usual historical pattern. With the passing of the destructive stage of the 1917 Revolution, criminality began rapidly to decrease, soon resuming its low prerevolutionary level.

From this negative barometer of morality let us turn to *positive* criteria, such as the degree of willingness to make *supreme sacrifices for others — especially for one's own country.* The unselfish and heroic sacrifice by millions of Russians, during the present war, of their most precious possession, their very life — a phenomenon typical, by the way, of the reaction of the nation to all similar crises in the past — furnishes incontrovertible evidence of the high ethical standards of the masses, which, according to this test, compare favorably with those of any other people. Furthermore, the sacrifices in question have been made in the prosecution of a *just* war — not in the interest of exploiting and enslaving other peoples, as in the case of the Nazis. Incidentally (as was pointed out in Chapter Two), the traditional policy of the government of Russia toward subject races (some of which were subjugated by force of arms) has been extraordinarily fair and generous. The dominant ethnic group, far from seeking for itself a maximum of privileges and a minimum of burdens, has borne its full quota of obligations and has frequently accorded the minor racial elements a disproportionately large share of benefits.

This spirit of sacrifice on behalf of the well-being of others and the preservation of major cultural values — a spirit signalized by fearless courage, unselfish devotion, and fortitude and endurance — has manifested itself in hundreds of ways — for example, in the conduct of doctors, teachers, and other professional workers who, on the whole, have performed their duties faithfully and well, at the expense of personal comfort, wealth, physical health, and other values. The Russian professional classes are justly regarded as among the least selfish in the entire world.

The same altruism has been evinced in dozens of objective institutionalized forms. The terms *mutual aid* and *co-operation* instantly suggest Russia as one of the first and most conspicuous exemplars of the activities in question. In Chapter Three, I indicated that the co-operative movement, both in the economic and in the cultural field, was as highly developed in Russia as in any leading nation, and possibly even more so. In the same chapter I referred to the mutual aid regularly practiced by the peasants in their day-to-day relations with one another. In P. Kropotkin's *Mutual Aid* can be found many other exemplifications of mutual aid as practiced in Russia. *Social service* and *charity,* in the form of both institutional and noninstitutional help extended to orphans, the poor and other unfortunates, furnish another token of the moral consciousness of a people. In Russia they have existed ever since the introduction of Christianity. Before the Revolution an entire government department — the so-called "Department of the Empress Mary" — was allotted to that purpose, in addition to the social and charitable institutions of the municipalities, provinces, *zemstvos,* and counties, and private associations. In an informal and spontaneous manner the phenomenon was manifested every day in millions of cases, especially among the peasants. However low might be the standard of living enjoyed by the peasants of a given village, as long as they possessed anything at all there was less likelihood of one's starving in the village than in many a large city in most countries of the world. To refuse to share food and other elementary necessities with even an unknown beggar was regarded as indecent. Such mores and folkways typical of the peasantry, who constituted approximately 85 per cent of the total population prior to the Revolution, speak for themselves. If a like spirit of compassion, helpfulness, and altruism had animated to the same extent the urban and industrialized centers of the world, there would have been far less of poverty, suffering, loneliness, and despair, as well as their tragic aftermath — namely, envy and hatred, crime and vice.

If now we survey *religion, philosophy, literature, and the fine arts* as mirrors of the moral standards of a people, according to this barometer as well Russia stands as high as any other nation. A spirit of universal love and compassion, as has been said, is their underlying principle or motif. In Russian literature and the fine arts, to say nothing of religion and philosophy, ethical problems have occupied a larger place than in the literature and fine arts of almost any other country since the middle of the nineteenth century. When one refers to literary works in which ethical problems are subjected to acute analysis, the names of Dostoevski and Tolstoi usually first come to mind. In the world literature of this epoch the most positive and exalted types of moral personality are depicted pre-eminently in the literature of Russia. Frivolity, ethical negativism and cynicism, the prostituting of moral values for commercial and kindred purposes, and unethical hedonism — these and kindred symptoms of low morality play a far less conspicuous role in the literature and fine arts of Russia than in those of most of the Western countries.

As regards such criteria as *faithfulness to international commitments and agreements,* no historian of diplomatic relations can possibly demonstrate that Russia has violated her obligations more frequently than other nations, or as frequently as some. Even the Soviet Government, since the passing of the destructive phase of the Revolution, has proved in this respect fully as reliable as any of the contemporary governments.

If, to multiply instances, we apply the ethical yardstick to *family life,* it will be found, as has been shown earlier, that the Russian family (apart from the first period of the Revolution) calls for no apology whatever.

Such values as *hospitality, sociality,* and *friendliness, hon-*

esty, industry, and the ordinary manifestations of *patience* and *perseverance* need not be dwelt on, since in all these respects the Russian people have generally elicited the praise of even casual foreign visitors.

Let us now consider specifically the ethical aspects of the *Russian Revolution.* When compared with other major revolutions, it exhibits one trait very significant for our purposes. Like all similar internal upheavals, to be sure, it led during its destructive stage to the profound demoralization of a considerable part of the population. But note this important difference. As in the case of the American Revolution, the armed forces did not invade, conquer, or annex foreign lands as did, for example, those of the French Revolutionaries, of Cromwell, or of Hitler or Mussolini. The virulence and disintegrative forces of the Russian Revolution were limited strictly to the domestic field. Moreover, certain possessions of Czarist Russia, like Manchuria and the Far-Eastern Railway with all the concessions appertaining thereto, were voluntarily returned to China by the Soviet Government, which likewise granted full sovereignty to Finland. This trait of the Revolution is highly symptomatic: it means that even if Russia was temporarily suffering from moral and social illness, she at least abstained from spreading the malady to other countries. She suffered (and still suffers) *alone* for her sins. Compare this with, for instance, the Nazi revolution, which, as soon as it had mustered sufficient strength, assaulted other nations with a view to their subjugation, exploitation, enslavement, or actual extermination by the most brutal and inhuman methods.

Again, Nazism has been aptly described as "the revolution of nihilism"— a characterization which in no way applies to the Russian Revolution, save possibly in the religious field. One may justifiably deplore the grave demoralization which the latter engendered; but this process was in no sense "nihilistic." Throughout its whole course it has been surcharged with intense ethical convictions and sentiments —

perverted, misguided, and pathological no doubt, but none the less idealistic. The supreme aim of the Revolution has been the world-wide annihilation of the capitalist system, with its exploitation and kindred injustices, and the poverty and misery arising therefrom. Likewise, the "dictatorship of the proletariat," while misguided, was nevertheless prompted by a thoroughly idealistic motive. The aims and objectives of the Russian anti-Communists as well were essentially ethical. Thousands who fought and perished on both the Communist and the anti-Communist side did so not so much for selfish purposes as in the interest of ideals and ethical values which, though perhaps perverted, were sincerely cherished. In all these respects the Russian Revolution was antipodal to the Nazi revolution.

Moreover, in spite of the enormous number of victims of the Russian Revolution, this number is negligible in comparison with the tens of millions of persons — mostly foreigners — already exterminated by the Nazis.

Finally, when one studies dispassionately the "ethics" of Nazism in relation to its practical consequences, particularly as regards the treatment of the invaded countries and their inhabitants, one can only conclude: if this is true morality, a crusade for the salvation of civilization and culture, then it is better to be as *anti*moral and *un*civilized as possible. For the Nazis have flouted every law, human and divine, and every moral value, including elementary decency. Consider the wholesale ruin they have spread over the world — the tens of millions of persons whom they have exterminated with the most cold-blooded and calculated efficiency. Remember their wanton destruction — just for the sake of destruction — of the cities and villages they had seized and were then forced to abandon in Russia. Recall how they have rounded up, like so many cattle, the able-bodied inhabitants, including even children, in the occupied regions of Russia, Poland, Czechoslovakia, the Balkans, France, and, in lesser degree, Holland

and Norway, driving them away by the hundreds of thousands to perform hard labor in Germany, separating parents from children and husbands from wives; how they have consigned hosts of women and girls to "mass brothels" for the gratification of their officers and soldiers; how they have massacred hundreds of thousands not for military or strategic considerations but merely for the satisfaction of their sadistic impulses or in order to obtain for themselves more *Lebensräum* through the removal of such "scum"; how they have killed wounded prisoners; how they have tortured or brutally maltreated in their prisons and concentration camps those who were not actually slaughtered; how they have delighted in the demolition or mutilation of historical and cultural monuments (buildings, documents, and the like); how they have everywhere left a train of poverty, famine, epidemics, and like calamities in their wake. It will then be abundantly evident that all the incursions of the barbarians of the past, not excluding those of Genghis Khan and Tamerlane and their Tatar hordes, were infinitely more humane and ethical than the Nazi "crusade for culture and civilization." It would, indeed, be difficult to find an adequate historical parallel for the destructive efficiency, the sadism, the bestiality and barbarity, of the Nazi invasion. To call it bestial or barbarous would, in fact, be an insult to the beasts and barbarians. Anyone who, like myself, witnessed for five years the worst misdeeds perpetrated by the Communist Revolution — and they were indeed terrible — is forced to conclude that the Communist brand of barbarism and bestiality is vastly preferable to that of the Nazis. The utter absurdity of Goebbels's propaganda is all the more patent in view of the fact that Hitler's invasion was launched at a time when the destructive stage of the Russian Revolution was at an end and Russia had already largely returned to her normal standards of morality and decency — of respect for human and divine laws, norms, and values. The Nazi "crusade" is thus seen to constitute one of the few cases of *utter and unmitigated moral degradation* in the history of the human race.

To sum up: judged by every accepted criterion of morality, Russia has proved throughout the course of her history to be as decent and law-abiding, self-sacrificing, and heroic as any of the foremost nations of the world.

2. *The United States*

The United States needs no particular defense in these respects. Even its worst enemies have never sought to indict it on the ground of moral inferiority. Instead they have resorted to the fiction of its domination by a "Wall-Street-Jewish plutocracy." Such a charge, by its very nature, condemns its accusers. To be sure, a certain element of plutocracy (as well as hypocrisy) is to be found in our social and political life. But what nation has ever been wholly free from this defect? The point to consider is therefore the comparative magnitude and quality of the phenomenon. From this standpoint the American plutocracy is possibly the most decent and creative in the whole world. If by "plutocrats" are meant captains of industry and finance (the Carnegies, Rockefellers, Fords, and the like), they have been the organizers of vast business empires beneficial to millions. When they have amassed a fortune, most of them have voluntarily dedicated a large part of their wealth to the service of the public (both in America and in foreign lands), creating, for example, huge foundations in the interest of science, philosophy, education, ethics, the fine arts, public health, and so forth. The same thing has been done, on a smaller scale, by the rank and file of the well-to-do. An exceptionally large proportion of social, philanthropic, religious, cultural, educational, scientific, and kindred enterprises have relied substantially upon the contributions of American "plutocrats," large and small. There is scarcely any other land in which a comparable development of socially beneficent "business empires" and a correspondingly generous return to society of the wealth amassed in the process of this economic empire building have occurred. A parallel case is afforded, incidentally, by Russia's nascent "plutocrats." While other countries have produced as many plutocrats, in proportion to their population, as this country, they have unfortunately failed to exhibit in like measure the virtues of the American "plutocracy." All too often they have made their money in socially less useful ways and have reserved it for themselves in larger measure than has the American business class. In the light of this comparison the American plutocracy is the most creative, the most generous, and the most highly moral among all the plutocracies in the world. If the official plutocracy of the Nazi and other dictatorial governments had shown even a small portion of the creativeness, inventiveness, organizing ability, and generosity typical of the American plutocratic class, the lot of their respective countries would have been much happier — their misery far less acute, their poverty far less tragic, and the human dignity of their subjects much more highly respected — than it is, for instance, under the yoke of such bloody plutocrats as Hitler, Goering, Goebbels, and their henchmen.

Another sin of which the United States is accused is *imperialism*. America is certainly not entirely free from this defect, any more than any other great power. But there are *imperialisms and imperialisms*. When the United States "imperialistically" entered the First World War and at the same time explicitly renounced all territorial or other selfish advantages, this represented *one* kind of "imperialism" radically different from that of Hitler's Germany, Mussolini's Italy, and many other great powers, which have seized everything they could lay their hands on, violating virtually every law, human and divine. Again, the United States was "imperialistic" in taking the Filipinos under its protection; in developing their political, social, and other institutions; and, finally, in voluntarily bestowing upon them unqualified freedom and national sovereignty. This kind of "imperialism" is, however, as radically different from that of its detractors — especially the Axis detractors — as heaven is different from hell. Since some type of imperialism seems to have hitherto been inevitable, one can hardly have any hesitation in preferring the American brand to practically all the others.

American *gangsterism* and *criminality* are often cited as further evidence of moral degeneracy. The accusation at once avoids a sound analysis of the phenomena in question and enormously exaggerates their magnitude. Objectively considered, American gangsterism proves to have been a purely temporary phenomenon, due to a special combination of circumstances and limited to a very small group of persons. Within a few years after its emergence, particularly after the abandonment of prohibition, it had largely disappeared. At present it is for the most part merely an unpleasant memory.

Moreover, when properly analyzed, the high index of American criminality is found to be largely attributable to such "crimes" as violation of the prohibition amendment and the traffic regulations, and similar offenses. The index of grave crimes in this country is about the same as that of most other highly industrialized societies, or at the worst only slightly higher.

This nation has been accused, furthermore, of *materialism;* but the indictment has never even remotely demonstrated precisely what is meant by the term or proved that materialism is more widespread in this country than elsewhere. In most cases the accusation turns out to be little more than a manifestation of envy of a prosperous neighbor on the part of those who are materially less well endowed. Still more naïve are certain other moral strictures, too childish to warrant serious consideration.

It should be borne in mind that *the total ethical physiog-*

nomy of a nation is made up of not only its negative but also its positive characteristics. When, side by side with the defects, the positive moral qualities of the American people are taken due account of, the decent, sometimes exceptionally altruistic, and occasionally heroic moral standards of the nation clearly emerge. Among the important ethical assets of our people are the following. First, there is the firm conviction that the ethical precepts of Christianity are eternally valid and cannot be replaced by any set of opposite principles. This assurance tends to prevent the nation from going seriously astray, as has happened to the Germans under the Nazi leadership and to the Russians during the destructive phase of the Revolution. The Americans may commit trespasses, but they do not deny the validity of the *Sermon on the Mount.* Secondly, there is the sincere conviction, formulated in the *Constitution* and applied to a considerable extent in actual social life, that ethically, in their moral dignity, all human beings are equal, and are hence entitled to respect, to being judged on their own merits, to equality of opportunity, and to a decent minimum of economic, educational, and cultural advantages. There is a deeply rooted ethos of freedom, as distinguished from licentiousness; a marked spirit of fairness in ethical and social relationships; a spirit of genuine tolerance toward different values when these are not positively immoral and socially harmful; a striving for the realization of international brotherhood (discussed in Chapter Three); a practical idealism and generosity (often unnoticed by superficial observers) running deep in the subsoil of American social life; an extraordinary development of spontaneous private philanthropy and of social service, on a scale hardly known in any other country; an equally conspicuous international relief work; and a relative absence of serious class hatred and class struggle. When these and other ethical and social traits are duly assessed, it is seen that, with all its defects, the United States calls for no apology.

The net conclusion of this chapter is that both nations exhibit at least as high moral standards as any other people. In respect to a number of specific ethical traits the two countries are mutually very congenial. Therefore in the field of ethical values, as in other fields, there is no fundamental antagonism or irreconcilability between Russia and the United States.

CHAPTER SEVEN

CREATIVE BLOSSOMING OF THE TWO NATIONS

1. *Unrivaled Progress*

Among the many resemblances between the two countries being compared there is one which is particularly noteworthy. This is *the striking rate of progress that both nations have experienced, particularly since the middle of the nineteenth century.* The progress has been so remarkable and the release of creative forces has been so great that both nations came of age in a very short span of time, during which the tempo and magnitude of their creativeness outstripped that of practically every other nation in the world. To be sure, there were nations, like Great Britain and Germany, which also advanced, but the tempo and magnitude of their progress remained notably lower than that of the United States and Russia. Other nations such as France merely maintained, and not too successfully at that, the standards of an earlier epoch, while certain empires, of which Austria is an example, showed signs of actual decline. Only the westernization of Japan might appear to be on a par with the cultural blossoming of the two nations being discussed. But this rapid Westernization of Japan consisted mainly in an imitative importation of Western technology, business methods, and the worst forms of imperialism, without any important contribution being made by Japan to those fields and without any conspicuous cultural renaissance in Japanese religion and ethics, philosophy and fine arts, mores and manners. In these cultural fields Japan either retained her traditional values or aped the West. These considerations indicate why the creative flowering of Russia and of the United States in the period considered has hardly been rivaled by any other nation.

Although the world has generally acknowledged the progress made by the United States during this period in economic, technological, and, to a lesser degree, in sociocultural accomplishments, it has failed to appreciate the comparable blossoming of Russia since the middle of the nineteenth century. The prevalent opinion is that Russia was stagnant and that this backwardness was the real cause of the Russian Revolution. This myth that stagnation and backwardness is the principal cause of revolutions is one of the particularly popular myths prevalent in the social sciences and among politicians and has won an almost universal acceptance. The real situation has been quite the reverse: revolutions typically occur not in a period of stagnation but rather in an era of very rapid transformation and change, often in the decades of an extraordinary renaissance of culture. This is true of Greece where the frequency of revolutions was at its peak during the fifth and fourth centuries B.C., which centuries were also the climax of Greek culture and creativeness. In Rome the same relationship prevailed: the most revolutionary centuries were the first B.C., the first A.D., and the third A.D., and these centuries, particularly the first B.C., and the first A.D., represented the zenith of Rome's sociocultural creativeness. Likewise the European Renaissance and the Reformation, extending from the thirteenth to the sixteenth centuries, were accompanied by internal disturbances throughout the continent on a scale exceeded only by the revolutions of the twentieth century.[1]

This prevalent, though not universal rule, is well exemplified by Russia and the Russian Revolution.[2] Let us briefly consider some salient features of Russia's remarkable progress which began somewhat after the middle of the nineteenth century and reached its culmination toward the close of that century and the beginning of the present century.

[1] See the detailed data in my *Social and Cultural Dynamics*, Vol. III.
[2] See N. S. Timasheff, "On the Russian Revolution," *Review of Politics*, July, 1942.

2. *Growth of the Russian Population*

Vitally and quantitatively the population of Russia increased from 67,000,000 in 1851 to 129,000,000 in 1897, and to 176,000,000 in 1914. This unprecedented rate of increase can not be attributed to any immigration and in only a very small measure was it due to the incorporation into Russia of new regions and populations. Primarily, it represents the natural growth of a population whose high birth rate has greatly exceeded its death rate. From this standpoint the growth of the Russian nation has been truly unique and can be matched by none of the great Western powers.

With the onset of the World War the trend was temporarily reversed. Throughout the war years, and particularly during the destructive period of the Revolution, from 1918 to 1922, there was an actual decline of population; instead of an average annual growth of about three million persons there was a loss of some thirteen to fifteen millions between 1918 and 1922, and of approximately twenty million persons over the longer period of 1914 to 1922. This reversal was due to the losses of life in the war and the Revolution and to a greatly increased death rate brought about by starvation, epidemics, and extreme hardships, and to a markedly curtailed birth rate. However, as soon as the worst destructive conditions had passed, the population of Russia showed a remarkable comeback in its vitality; after 1923 the death rate fell considerably, the birth rate rose to its prerevolutionary level, and the rapid growth of the population resumed its prerevolutionary trend. The net reproduction ratio of post-revolutionary Russia has been higher (1.70) than in any other country in the world. (Most countries have a ratio ranging from .67 to 1.5.)

Qualitatively, the health and vitality of the Russian population has been one of the best in the world. Medical examinations of school children and of the recruits for the armed forces of Russia (with its universal military duty), as well as other tests of the health of the population have shown, for this period, with the exception of the destructive period of the Revolution, a comparatively high level of the health and vitality of the bulk of the Russian population, so far as the congenital diseases are concerned. It remains one of the most robust and inherently vital populations in the whole world, in spite of the fact that it has lived under harder and possibly less sanitary conditions than those of many nations of the West.

If the present low birth rate of Western countries persists, and if Russia continues to maintain its exceptionally high rate of natural increase, it is clear that Russia will not only grow in man power but her population is likely to supplant more and more the stationary or dwindling populations of the West. If we consider further that periods of depopulation have usually been followed by a decline in the culture of the country concerned the enormous consequences of this disparity in the future must be clear to every intelligent person. The naïvely optimistic suppositions made by partisans of birth control that a low birth rate correlates with a cultural efflorescence is not borne out by historical facts, as the classical case of Greco-Roman population decline demonstrates conclusively.

3. *Sociopolitical Progress of Russia*

Russia has traversed a considerable distance during the last ninety years in its *sociopolitical* structure. It was an unlimited monarchy at the beginning of the period, changed to a constitutional monarchy in 1906, transformed itself in 1917, even before the Communist Revolution, to a federative republic, and finally became organized as a Union of Soviet Republics.

It was in this same period that Russia, by a law of 1861, *rid itself of the social and ethical cancer of serfdom.* From a society legally and factually composed of several *hierarchical orders* beginning with a nobility and ending with the peasantry, each order having different ranks, privileges, and duties, Russia became a society in which *all citizens were equal* by law and had an equal opportunity for realization of their talents and abilities (reforms of 1861, 1886, 1905-8, 1917). Step by step both legal and factual inequalities between the several orders or classes were abolished. The nobility received its death blow through the reforms of 1861 and subsequent years. Since that time it has been socially and legally dying out. Its main wealth has always been land, and that residue which was left to it after the liberation of the serfs in 1861 was rapidly passing into the hands of the peasantry. On the eve of the Revolution of 1917 a mere eight to ten per cent of all the cultivated lands of Russia remained in the hands of the old nobility; this is less than the proportion of cultivated land held by the upper and middle (nonfarming) classes in most of the countries of the West. Superficial writers on Russia generally assert that prior to the Revolution nearly all the land was in the hands of the nobility and that it was the Revolution which really gave the land to the peasants. The fallacy of this myth must be evident in the light of the foregoing considerations; the Revolution added very little to the land of the peasants. In all other rights, too, the peasants were made the equals of other citizens well before the Revolution and to such an extent that after 1906 the expression "peasant" no longer referred to a special order in Russia and began to mean as in this country, an agricultural occupation or agricultural class.

During the same period Russia passed from a condition of *limited freedom to one characterized by all the main freedoms of press, meetings, religion, associations, unions, and so on, found in democratic countries.* After the Constitution of 1906 these were all introduced and practiced to an extent in some respects greater than in many other countries. Current notions as to the tyranny of the Czarist regime have some basis insofar as they are applied to the period before 1861 and in a much smaller degree between 1861 and 1906. After that the principal vice of the Czarist regime was not its despotism and tyranny but its incompetence, softness, and impotence. It was criticized openly in the press, in public meetings, in the *Duma* (the Russian Parliament), in university lectures and so on, and much more sharply and scathingly than the American Government is criticized by its bitterest opponents. If criticism were directed against the American Government with the same severity that the Czarist regime was criticized in Russia, our sensibilities would be violently shocked. The same considerations pertain to the so-called cruelty of the Czarist Government towards its political opponents. Socialist and revolutionary bodies, including the Social-Revolutionary, the Social-Democratic, and the Communist parties had their representatives and factions in the *Duma*, openly and legally. All these parties, not to mention milder oppositional political groups, legally published their newspapers, magazines, and books after 1906. In brief, liberty of press and thought in Russia after 1906 was about as extensive as in most of the democratic countries. Its typical impotence, mixed with an inconsistent humanitarianism, marked even the penal policy of the old regime, especially after 1906. This applied as much to political crimes such as revolutionary activity as it did to ordinary crimes. A significant index of this humanitarianism is the fact that no death penalty existed, even for murder of the first degree, since the middle of the eighteenth century. It is true that capital punishment was meted out in cases of attempts to murder the Czar or an immediate member of the Czarist family, or when acts of violence were committed during martial law. But this kind of sanction for a crime against the life of a president or king or for violence during martial law is a rule in all democratic countries, the United States not excluded. Even in crimes such as these a certain compassion and sympathy for the murderer was sometimes manifested by representatives of the Czarist family to an extent inconceivable anywhere else. The attitude displayed by the wife of the Grand Duke Sergius toward her husband's murderer, Kalliaiev, is a case in point. On occasions when such crimes were decided by a jury, a complete acquittal would sometimes be given the political murderer. The story of a famous revolutionary Vera Zassoulitch, who murdered a governor-general during martial law, furnishes an example of this: she was found not guilty and was exonerated although her defence did not deny at all that she had committed the murder. In other respects political criminals were treated by the old regime of the twentieth century in a remarkably mild manner. With a slight exaggeration one can say that the banishment and imprisonment of political offenders was more in the nature of granting them a vacation, with most of the expenses paid. As a matter of fact university professors frequently looked upon imprisonment in just this manner; we used to say that in prison or in the province of banishment, we would have plenty of time to do our studies and research. And indeed many studies and books were completed under precisely these conditions.[3] Once in a while through the indiscreet action of this or that official some third degree method would be applied, but such abuses will be found in any penal system. They were the exception and not the rule. Political prisoners were carefully segregated from usual criminals and were treated in a wholly different manner.

[3] I was imprisoned three times by the old regime. In the first imprisonment (in Kineschma, Kostroma Province) we were free to go into the office of the prison warden to use its telephone and other facilities; as a matter of fact we very quickly turned the prison into one of the safest places for keeping the fiery revolutionary literature in the whole city. Similar conditions prevailed in my other imprisonments by the Czarist regime. In contrast to these, the imprisonment by the Soviet regime in the years 1918-1922 were infinitely worse. We were treated in the most brutal manner; some of my political comrades, like Professors Kokoshkin and Shingareff (ministers in the Kerensky government) were murdered by a Bolshevist guard in the prison-hospital; our lives were incessantly menaced. Czarist prisons were a paradise in comparison with the Communist infernos.

The widespread notion that extreme cruelty characterized the penal measures of the old regime — an idea popularized by Kennan's and other works — has some basis of fact when it is applied to the later nineteenth century. But even then they were anachronisms and nothing more.[4] In brief, the main defect of the dying Czarist regime was not cruelty and tyranny but merely impotence, vacillation, and stupidity. After 1906 the Czarist regime was moribund and expiring steadily. Even had there been no revolution the old regime would have been either abolished or transformed into a liberal monarchy somewhat after the British pattern in which a king reigns but does not rule.

To sum up, Russia made up for her previous "backwardness and lethargy" by evolving in a remarkably short span of time a sociopolitical system that was in a real sense the equal of the democratic systems of most republics. Had there been no World War I the whole transition of Russia to the status of one of the most free, prosperous, and creative nations would have been accomplished peacefully, without any revolution. It was the very rapidity of Russia's reconstruction process that rendered the nation unstable and susceptible to every perturbation. The great war unsettled this delicate equilibrium and terminated in revolution.

The first period of the Communist Revolution was characterized by a gross retrogression — a feature that marks every great revolution. Basic freedoms and liberties were obliterated, and an unlimited dictatorship by the Communist rulers displaced the democratic republican regime established by the Kerenski Government. Elemental rights of man and of citizen were trampled upon. Neither security of life nor any other right was respected. All the enemies of the Communist Government and even persons remotely suspected as opponents

---

[4] I am stating this not only on the basis of my personal experiences but also as a professor of criminal law and procedure — my first specialty before I shifted to sociology.

were butchered, banished, or imprisoned. There was, in short, *a regime of unlimited terror and butchery*. Fortunately, with the passing of the destructive phase of the Revolution this regime of government by mass terror gradually waned. The Revolution had annihilated, step by step, the privileged and rich, then the middle classes, and finally the Communists themselves in successive purges. There simply remained no further groups to extinguish. By 1940 the ameliorative process had progressed far, though it still had not restored prerevolutionary privileges. With the inception of World War II new conditions appeared which altered the whole Russian scene, as it did that of every other nation involved in this desperate and terrible struggle. The present regime in Russia is, of course, the regime of martial law, in which one can scarcely expect to find mildness, liberalism, and humanitarianism. But the stern regime that arises out of *national necessity* is a very different thing from the terroristic regime of Communism. When the war is over, this regime of martial law will give place to the prerevolutionary regime of political, economic, and social democracy, even more just and ennobled than the old regime had been after its reforms.

Thus we see that Russia indeed traversed an enormous distance in the field of sociopolitical reconstruction during a short period of some ninety years. More than that: in this as well as in other fields *the Russian nation has displayed conspicuously its creative forces*. Russia has demonstrated, first, that great social reforms could be carried through by her in an *orderly and peaceful manner*. The great social reforms of 1861 and subsequent years represent some of the most brilliant and successful experiments in peaceful reform that have ever been made. They remodeled Russia, politically, economically, socially, culturally, and morally, from the top to the bottom, without any bloodshed and without any internal disturbances. As such the achievement has been justly known to historians as "the Great Reform." It demonstrates that

Russia is as capable as any nation of accomplishing great social reconstructions in an orderly and peaceful manner. These reforms, moreover, were original; they were not a mere imitation of the institutions of other countries: such achievements as the creation of a new legal and judicial system; of the *zemstvo;* and of a number of other cultural institutions were original in many respects.

Still greater originality has been manifested by Russia in the creation of its *Soviet regime.* However destructive and terrible were the atrocities of the Revolution in its initial Communist phase — which show, if nothing else, that Russia is certainly capable of staging as great a revolution as mankind has ever known — *the Soviet regime appears unmistakably as one of the four most original experiments that have been made since the close of the eighteenth century in the creation of new sociopolitical systems. The first of these truly original creations was the democratic republican form of government, as developed by the United States and by revolutionary France. The second great invention was Anglo-Saxon: the creation of the free commonwealth of nations* which has been evolved by Great Britain during the last three decades and which is still being perfected. *The third great experiment was the League of Nations and the Hague International Court, both of which attempts have so far been only partially successful.* Finally, *the fourth great experiment is the Soviet regime.* Divested of the bloody methods which led to its establishment, and taken at its intrinsic value, it is certainly one of the most radical and original sociopolitical innovations. It aims to create not only political but also economic and sociocultural democracy; it seeks to eliminate exploitation and injustice far more radically than have the regimes of purely political democracies. It attempts to combine the advantages of modern technological centralization, large scale production, and management with autonomy of the local groups; to merge the benefits of collectivism with those of freedom, self-expression, and individual initiative; to reconcile the most despotic governmental bureaucracy with freedom; to integrate social planning with spontaneity and creative deviation; to compromise radical equality with inequality of merit and talent; and to harmonize the responsibility of a society for each of its members with the responsibility of an individual to himself and to the society.

So far the regime has failed in some of these tasks, but in some others it has shown a great vitality and promise of success. It "hit" something that is on the agenda of history. This is the reason why it not only succeeded in establishing itself in Russia but also why it has spread and has been imitated by many other countries in a modified form. The clearest case of this is to be found in Fascism and Nazism. In spite of all their "crusades" against Soviet Russia, both of these systems are but imitative variations upon the Soviet model; both of them borrowed from it all their essential characteristics, often to the minutest detail, *generally failing to borrow the main virtues and succeeding in assimilating all the vices of the Soviet system.* In this sense the Soviet system is the parent of these two abortive children.[5] Other features of the Soviet system like "integral social planning," an enormous expansion of the governmental regulation, technologically rationalized centralization of industrial management, extension of democracy into the economic field, "freedom from want," and securing to everyone a decent minimum of economic and sociocultural conditions, have all spread and diffused over many countries through the impetus of the Soviet experiment. Finally, the very popularity of the Soviet system among the masses of mankind throughout the world further testifies to the distinctive originality of the system. These considerations give reason for supposing that the Soviet system contains

[5] Any competent historian of these regimes knows that the Soviet system was systematically studied — and then imitated — by Nazism in a great many ways. Thus, the Gestapo was organized in close imitation of the Cheka. The same is true, to a lesser degree, of Fascism.

fruitful and creative ingredients that are destined to live in the history of men's great sociopolitical experiments. Thus we see clearly in this field an extraordinary unfolding of the creative forces of Russia during the period considered. The greatest sociopolitical innovation of the twentieth century so far belongs unquestionably to Russia.

4. Economic, Industrial, and Technological Progress of Russia

At the present time even the man in the street knows something about the remarkable technological, industrial, and economic progress which Russia has made during the three successive five-year plans. Most people do not realize, however, that this progress is not something that has suddenly and for the first time appeared in Russia. Actually it is but the logical continuation of a trend that began in the middle of the nineteenth century, gathered momentum during subsequent decades, and became conspicuous around the end of the nineteenth century and in the prewar twentieth century. It was interrupted by World War I and by the destructive phase of the Revolution, but with the end of this destructive period it reappeared in the form of the five-year plans with their celebrated achievements.[6] In this we find further corroboration of the generalization that any great revolution following its destructive phase, merely revives and continues the broad trends of the prerevolutionary period.

Let us consider a few facts that reveal this economic progress.

Around the middle of the nineteenth century the *cotton* in-

---

[6] It is worth noting that the old regime and more especially the Kerensky regime had laid down plans for a rapid industrialization of Russia and had arranged for their consummation, well before the Soviets. The Soviet government took the "blueprints" of its five-year plans from its predecessors and, with modification, realized them.

dustry in Russia was practically nonexistent. By 1905 it already employed 7,350,683 spindles and 178,506 looms. By 1914 it had about 9,000,000 spindles and 250,000 looms, making it the fourth largest cotton industry in the world, exceeded only by that of the United States, Great Britain, and Germany. By 1940 Russia's cotton industry occupied about the second place in the world.

The *metallurgical* industry in 1900 produced 91,000,000 puds (a pud represents about 40 English pounds); in 1914 its output was 223,700,000 puds. By 1940 the Russian metallurgical industry was second in the world, the first place belonging to the United States.

The *oil* industry of the Baku area produced in 1860 some 2,500,000 puds; in 1905 it produced 455,900,000 puds, in 1913, 561,300,000 puds. By 1940 Russia occupied second place in the world in this field too. Similarly the *coal* industry increased its output threefold in the period from 1900 to 1914. The production of *sugar, tobacco, alcohol,* and *flour* likewise increased from three to four and five times within the period of 1900 to 1914.

In 1860 Russia had only 660 miles of *railroads*. By 1912 the total length of Russian railroads increased up to 40,194 miles; by 1914 to 49,000 miles, making Russia's railroad system second only to that of the United States. By 1940 it practically rivaled the railroad system of the United States in total mileage. One unit of this system is the Trans-Siberian Railroad, built in the period from 1892 to 1905, and which is 5,542 miles long — the longest railroad in the world. Like the great American transcontinental lines the Trans-Siberian railway was pushed through stupendous natural obstacles and has been rightly called one of the most daring railroad projects of the world. Taken as a whole, in the period from 1890 to 1913, *the total production of Russian large scale industry quadrupled,* increasing in value from 1.5 billion gold rubles to 6 billion.

Equally great strides were made in the field of *agriculture*. Following the liberation of the serfs, 148 million hectares of arable land were distributed to the peasants of European Russia, while 89 million hectares remained in the hands of the landlords and 8 million in the hands of the State. By 1914 there remained only some 30 to 35 million hectares in the landlords' possession, the remainder passing to the peasantry. This transition went on with an accelerated tempo in the period from 1900 to 1914, with fully as great a transfer of land to the peasants as had taken place during the preceding forty years. Of the 30 to 35 million hectares remaining in the hands of the landlords by 1914, a considerable part passed into the hands of the peasants between the years 1914 and 1917. Consequently, on the eve of the Revolution a mere 8 to 10 per cent of the arable land was still in the hands of other classes than the peasantry. The Russian Revolution only completed this process which, as we see, was practically terminated before the Revolution. This indicates once more the gross inaccuracy of the widespread idea that the peasants received their land from the Revolution and that before it they had hardly any land at all.

The *area of cultivated land* also rapidly expanded from 92,690,000 *desiatens* in 1905 to 109,670,000 *desiatens* in 1914. The *average crop* of the peasant land almost doubled in value during the period considered. Likewise livestock production rose appreciably; the number of horses increased from 25 million in 1895 to 36 million in 1916; the number of horned cattle from 31 million to 61 million in 1916.

Similarly the *budgets of the central* as well as of *the local governments grew rapidly*, reflecting the economic development of the country. The expenditures of the central government amounted to 1,889,000,000 rubles in 1900 and 3,382,-000,000 in 1913, of which only one quarter was used for the army, navy, and the defence of the country, the rest being expended for economic and cultural purposes. The total expenditure of all the *zemstvo* in thirty-four provinces of Russia was in 1875 28,870,000 rubles; in 1905, 124,185,000; in 1914, 400,000,000 rubles.

At the beginning of the twentieth century there was hardly any co-operative organization to speak of. But by 1915 Russia had approximately 33,000 co-operative societies with a total membership of some 13,000,000, most of whom were peasants.

Likewise *the standard of living* as well as *the national wealth* of the Russian nation was rising rapidly, especially during the period 1900 to 1914. An eminent English economist and statistician, A. L. Bowley, rightly remarks that at the end of the nineteenth and in the prewar twentieth century the greatest real increase of the national wealth and income per capita was precisely in the United States and in Russia; while in other countries such as Great Britain, "the average incomes were one third greater in 1913 than in 1880" and even here "the increase was gained principally before 1900, since when it barely kept pace with the diminishing value of money." [7]

During the World War I [8] and especially during the destructive period of the Revolution the standard of living and per capita income declined greatly in Russia as it did in most of the belligerent countries: from an average per capita income of 101.35 gold rubles in 1913, it fell to 85.60 in 1916-1917, and to 40 gold rubles in 1922-1923. With the passing of the destructive period of the Revolution it began to rise and continued rising up to 1940 when the invasion of Russia precipitated the present devastating war and temporarily disrupted the trend.

[7] A. L. Bowley, *The Change in the Distribution of the National Income,* 1880-1913 (Oxford University Press, 1920), p. 26 et passim.

[8] Indeed, this rapid progress of Russia was one of the very reasons for the invasion of Russia in 1914 (as well as in 1941) by German forces: the German general staff rightly considered it imperative to strike at Russia early, for with the passing of every year Russia was developing militarily, economically, and culturally at an increasingly rapid rate, and was thereby becoming annually less and less liable to be defeated and more and more formidable as a possible enemy.

A rapid urbanization of Russia began around the middle of the nineteenth century and became increasingly marked toward the close of the century and during the twentieth century. The urbanization of Siberia and Manchuria bears a striking resemblance to the corresponding process in the United States. A number of comparatively large cities like Kharbin in Manchuria, which was founded and built by Russians, reached the 100,000 mark within a mere ten or fifteen years. This process became especially feverish in the reconstructive phase of the Revolution, when large industrial centers literally sprouted like mushrooms in every section of the country, including even the hitherto uninhabited Arctic and desert regions.

To sum up: the foregoing considerations demonstrate, first, that since the end of the nineteenth century, Russia was making a remarkable economic progress exceeded only by that of the United States; second, that this progress began several decades before the Revolution, and accelerated progressively from the middle of the nineteenth century to the twentieth century; third, that the spectacular technological and economic progress of Russia after the termination of the destructive period of the Revolution was not an initiation but rather a resumption and continuation of the trend that existed before the Revolution.

As a result, by 1940 Russia became in all essential respects the second most industrialized and technologized country in the *world*, producing from 20 to 25 per cent of the *world's* iron ores; 15 to 20 per cent of the *world's* petroleum; 10 to 12 per cent of the coal output of the world; 10 to 12 per cent of water power; 8 to 10 per cent of copper; 65 to 70 per cent of manganese; 45 to 50 per cent of rye; 25 to 30 per cent of wheat; 35 to 40 per cent of phosphates; 10 to 12 per cent of cotton; 35 to 40 per cent of hemp; 75 to 80 per cent of flax; 13 to 15 per cent of gold; 20 to 22 per cent of linseed; 3 to 5 per cent of wool; 3 to 5 per cent of zinc, lead, and nickel; and occupying first or second place in the world in the production of artificial rubber.

All in all, by 1940 only the United States of America exceeded Russia in industrial output in its tempo and magnitude of economic and technological development. When the war is over and if a period of lasting peace is granted to Russia and to mankind as a whole, there is not a slightest doubt that this rapid economic progress of Russia will be resumed, in spite of the gigantic and terrible destruction of life, cities, industrial centers, agriculture, and economic wealth which this war is wreaking upon Russia. The nation has the means, the resources, the brains, the energy, and everything else that is necessary for such a revival. Besides, it has the call of destiny for this task. When any nation is in such a position, nothing, not even the most terrible destruction of war and revolution, can deter it in the fulfillment of its manifest destiny.

5. *Educational and Cultural Progress of Russia*

Even more remarkable has been the progress of Russia in the field of cultural endeavor. Such advance is evidenced by the rapid spread of education and medical care throughout the country, and especially by a unique burst of cultural creativeness in the highest levels of achievement. Here are a few summary data on the main features of this progress.

If we were to believe most of the judgments passed on Russian education by foreign writers, radio commentators, and newspaper reporters we would be led to suppose that Russia, before the Revolution, was quite illiterate and that literacy, schools, science, technology, and inventions appeared in Russia only with the Revolution. According to this prevalent "philosophy of history" the Revolution, in one magical stroke, by a sudden "presto," created in a few years almost universal literacy, and established schools and universities *ex nihilo*. Likewise according to this philosophy of history the Revolution created by its magical "presto" freedom, liberty, economic progress, and so on wholly by itself. Needless to say, this kind of theory of social progress is perfectly silly and reflects the ignorance of its proponents.

Just as in other fields, the *rapid spread of literacy and education* in Russia began very shortly after the reforms of 1861, gathering momentum in subsequent decades up to 1917. Then for a few years the trend was halted by the destructive phase of the Revolution, but was resumed again and continued after the destructive phase had passed. Before 1861 the bulk of the Russian population was illiterate and the number of the primary schools for peasant and labor classes was insignificant, indeed almost nonexistent. In 1881 the number of pupils in elementary public schools was 1,141,000; in 1903, 5,237,000; in 1915, 8,147,000. This number does not include the considerable number who were educated either at home or in privileged private schools.

Parallel with this increase of schools and pupils *the percentage of literacy* grew rapidly. Among the recruits taken into the armed forces (military duty was obligatory and universal in Russia) the percentage of literate recruits, i.e., those able to read and write, was 21.98 in 1874-1883; 43.75 in 1894-1903; and 62.62 in 1904-1913. The percentage of children of school age who had actually received primary school education was 45 per cent in 1905, and 70 per cent in 1914. In 1916 the *Duma* (Russian Parliament) passed a law which appropriated the necessary funds to make elementary education universal, with the aim of making all children of school age literate by 1919. Thus, even if there had been no revolution, a 100 per cent literacy for children of school age would have been achieved by 1919! These data show clearly the absurdity of the current opinion regarding literacy and illiteracy in prerevolutionary Russia. We see that the progress of literacy made enormous strides especially in the twentieth century and that before the Revolution at least 70 per cent of the children had had an elementary school education and were able to read. The Revolution in its destructive years disrupted the trend and threw the country back in this respect. But with the destructive phase over, the earlier trend reappeared and made very rapid progress up to 1940, so fast indeed that by that year practically 100 per cent of the children of school age and a large proportion of previously illiterate adults had become literate. In 1940 all in all some 40,000,000 pupils and students were attending schools of every type in Russia, beginning with the primary schools and ending with the universities. In other words one out of every four persons in Russia was attending a school of some kind.

Thus in this field of culture Russia reached the same level as all the other literate nations in the world.

Similar rapid progress was made in the *field of secondary and college education* for the period considered. By the middle of the nineteenth century there were very few secondary (high) schools and these few were accessible almost exclusively to the privileged classes. By 1894 the number of pupils in public secondary schools had become 225,000 and by 1914, 820,000. The number of students of both sexes in universities and colleges and in the highest technological, legal, and medical institutes was a mere handful before 1861 and most of these were from the privileged classes; in 1894 the number was about 15,000; in 1912, 137,000.[9] The figures speak for

[9] Russian universities and higher institutions of learning were all first-class universities and institutions capable before the Revolution of competing with the standards of the best universities in the world. They were notably different in their standards from many of our so-called colleges, universities, and institutions which in fact do not belong to the category of higher institutions of learning. In Russia all such institutions were called "*technicums*" or comparable names and were sharply separated from real universities and higher institutions of learning. If the pupils of such "*technicums*" were included in the indicated number of students, it would increase several times.

themselves.[10] Among the students the proportion coming from the peasant, laboring, and poorer classes consistently increased. By 1914 hardly less than 50 per cent of the students were from these classes. Russian universities and higher institutions granted a considerable number of scholarships and fellowships to the more capable students from the poorer classes. It may be added, by the way, that in their administration and control universities and institutions were more democratic than the American universities: the rector or president and the deans were all elected by the professorial body for short terms of two to four years. The president was thus only a temporary administrator. All university affairs were decided by the faculty and by student representatives. There was no all-powerful "board of trustees" or "regents" or "corporations" to rule the universities. Likewise all the professors and instructors were elected, on a competitive basis, by the faculty. In brief, Russian universities, before the Revolution, possessed extraordinarily great autonomy and were truly self-governing bodies.

The first years of the Revolution created an enormous number of "sham universities" and "sham secondary schools." Their standards were so low that secondary and university education was nearly ruined, not to speak of the deterioration in elementary education. In its more constructive period the Revolution resumed the interrupted trend and extended it a considerable distance. As on the eve of the Revolution secondary and university education was now open to all who desired it and were capable of absorbing it. By 1940 the number of students in all types of universities and colleges reached 600,000; that of students in technical schools, 700,000. If we add the students in certain other institutions and in correspondence courses the total number amounts to about

---

[10] For the sake of comparison we may note that in the United States, between 1815 and 1920, there were granted 496,618 college degrees.

2,000,000. These Soviet figures are probably somewhat inflated; it is reasonably certain also that the standards of learning and teaching in many of these "universities," "colleges," and "technical institutes" are considerably lower than they were in the true universities and technical institutes prior to the Revolution. Nevertheless, with all these qualifications the great progress made by higher education in Russia during the post-destructive period of the Revolution is unquestionable. Just as in other fields, the post-destructive period of the Revolution resumed and extended further the prerevolutionary trend.

To sum up: in all types of education and schooling Russia again made remarkable progress during the last ninety years of its history. If before the middle of the nineteenth century the Russian nation was lagging far behind other Western countries, in the twentieth century she made up the difference and at the present time need apologize to no other country in this field of culture.

Before entering upon a consideration of the flowering of cultural creativeness on the highest levels let us deliberate for a moment upon such cultural items as *medical care* and *social insurance*. During the years of my life abroad and in the United States I have read many times, frequently in the works of notable authorities on these matters, statements to the effect that before the Revolution there was hardly any medical care or social insurance at all in Russia, and that these services, particularly free and universally accessible state medical care, were created for the first time by the Revolution. I have even seen photographs of splendid hospitals which, according to the supposed experts, were built by the Soviet Government, but which I had seen standing and functioning before the Revolution. In other words, our so-called experts have once again been foisting upon the public ostensible "scientific facts" regarding medical care in Russia which are in reality nothing but pure myths.

The real situation was briefly as follows. First, public medical care through State, *zemstvo,* and other public bodies, free of charge and accessible to all, was introduced in Russia a long time ago; it was the principal system of medical care prior to the Revolution, for private doctors and hospitals comprised but an insignificant portion of Russian medical services. Second, this public system was in no sense cheap or second-rate, nor was it at all inferior in quality, personnel, and hospital facilities to the private system of medical care but was fully as good as the latter. As a matter of fact most of the doctors, particularly the great and distinguished ones, were "public doctors" who received their salaries from the State, *zemstvo,* and other public institutions. Only a small fraction of these had supplementary private practices. Third, before 1861 there was hardly any public medical care for the population, especially for the great masses of the people. In 1914 not only the cities but all the rural territories as well were being served by public hospitals and dispensaries created by the *zemstvo,* State, and other local and municipal agencies. The average radius of the rural medical district was about ten miles. In the forty provinces of Russia having *zemstvo* there were in 1914 thirty-three hundred medical districts in charge of *zemstvo* alone, not to mention the hospitals, dispensaries, and doctors that were in charge of the State and other public agencies.

To sum up: on the eve of the Revolution medical care was accessible to everyone in Russia who needed it and it was free from any charges. This covered hospitalization, doctors' services, and medicines. The system was really one of the best in the world, both in the quality of its service and in its accessibility to all. It is only within recent years that many Western countries, including the United States, have begun to adopt the principles of "socialized" medicine and medical care that were in operation several decades ago in Russia.

The Revolution, in its post-destructive phase, only continued this historical tradition of Russia, achieving, to be sure, considerable further progress by 1940. At that time there were 13,500 rural medical centers, with 20,000 doctors and 39,500 assistant doctors. So much for this aspect of cultural advance.

If we turn now to *social security and state social insurance* provisions, such as workers' accident insurance, and the like, we find that these were introduced in Russia by laws passed in 1903 and 1912. These were public programs in the same sense as our own Federal or State social security acts. Certain provisions were not covered, notably old age and unemployment insurance, but these were in process of formulation when the war brought them to an abrupt end in 1914. Health insurance was of course rendered unnecessary by the universal free medical system whose features we have already discussed. The Soviet regime, after passing through its initial destructive phase restored and further developed the programs that had been interrupted — at least, so far as the financial resources of the country permitted. By 1940 every one in Russia was at least in principle insured against the consequences of unemployment, sickness, accidents, and other such calamities; to a considerable extent the factual situation conformed to this principle. "Freedom from want" and a decent minimum of the necessities of life was proclaimed to be the right of every citizen. Actual realization of this "fourth freedom" was somewhat compromised by an inadequacy of the necessary resources but with the improvement of productive facilities the amplitude of its realization was slowly progressing. In this respect, far from lagging behind the Western countries, Russia was, on the eve of the present war, somewhat in advance of them.

Still more remarkable was the unfolding of *cultural creativeness during the nineteenth and twentieth centuries in the fields of science, technological invention, philosophy, law, fine arts, and especially in literature, music, drama, and paint-*

ing. In several of these fields Russia set the pace for the rest of the world.

In the field of *natural science* the period is marked by the rapid growth of a large body of first-class scientists — professors and researchers fully as competent as those of any other country. Especially after the reforms of 1861 Russian scientists were well abreast of the developments being made abroad in their fields. This is in contrast to the ignorance of Western scientists as to what Russian investigators were doing. Within this ever-growing body of scientists a large number of talented discoverers and creators made outstanding contributions to their respective fields, again only in small part recorded in the annals of science in the West. Finally, as we approach the twentieth century we find that with increasing frequency Russia is producing such outstanding leaders in science as Lobachevski in mathematics, Mendelyeev in chemistry, and I. Pavlov in the physiology of the nervous system and in psychology, to mention only a few names. On the eve of the Revolution Russian natural science could boast of an eminence second to none in the rest of the world.

The same is even more true of the *humanistic and social sciences.* History, economics, law, political science, sociology, philology, anthropology, psychology, and other disciplines flourished quantitatively and qualitatively as evidenced by the originality, solidity, brilliancy, and thoroughness of the works created in them. Most of the Russian works in these fields still remain wholly or largely unknown abroad. One manifestation of this high level of Russian scholarship is the readiness with which many of its representatives, forced to become refugees as a result of the Revolution, were given appointments by American and European universities, research institutes, and laboratories, and rose quickly to positions of international prominence in their respective fields.

Russian *philosophy,* likewise little known abroad, became

highly creative and original during the second part of the nineteenth century and in the twentieth century. Even such main currents of Western philosophy as materialism, Marxianism, positivism, empiricism, Hegelianism, Neo-Kantianism, and so on, were cultivated in Russia by men whose pre-eminence was certainly as great, if not greater, than that of the leading philosophers in most of the Western countries. In the field of philosophy Russia need apologize to no other country for its accomplishments.

Likewise in the field of *law,* in addition to the remarkable codification of Russian law achieved by Speranski in the first quarter of the nineteenth century, as well as several later codes, both civil and criminal, that were enacted during the nineteenth century and the prerevolutionary twentieth century, the whole field of the history and theory of law and ethics flowered in Russia to an extent unmatched in most of the Western countries.

Finally, as we have already seen, *technological inventiveness* and *applied science,* such as agronomy and medicine, began a vigorous development toward the close of the nineteenth century and the early twentieth century. Hand in hand with this development of natural science, technology, and industrialization, Russia became more and more "gadget-minded." The result was an increase in the number of applied inventions in all fields of human endeavor. In 1900 Russia alone accounted for some three or four per cent of all the inventions in the world, and by 1914 this percentage had doubled. Some of the inventors, having become refugees as a result of the Revolution, made significant contributions to the countries in which they have settled. Such names as Sikorski, Zworykin, Timoshenko, Ipatiev, and other eminent Russian inventors have become well known in the United States, their adopted land.

This efflorescence of science and technology was, of course, radically curtailed during the destructive years of the Revolution. As a result of execution, persecution, banishment, death by starvation and disease, and finally through an exodus of the scientists and inventors from Russia, the process was temporarily halted and thrown back. However, with the catastrophic phase of the Revolution terminated it re-emerged and continued its prerevolutionary trend. By 1940 the natural sciences, technology, and, in a less degree, the humanistic, social, philosophical, and juridical sciences (more limited in their freedom of thought and research than the "politically neutral" natural sciences) were successfully approaching their prerevolutionary level of creativeness and progress. Russian mathematics and astronomy, physics and chemistry, biology and medicine, agronomy and technology were by that time expanding rapidly. With a considerable basis in fact Russia was becoming known as "the nation of inventors." The present war has somewhat disrupted the process, intensifying it in certain fields, curtailing it in others. When the war has ended there is hardly any doubt that the great élan of scientific and technological, social science, juridical, and philosophical creativeness will be resumed and will be raised to even higher levels: its progress in Russia since the middle of the nineteenth century has so far been only a beginning.

In the fields of *literature, music, drama, and to a lesser degree painting,* Russia assumed *the foremost position in the world* during the period being considered. The greatest literature in the world since the first quarter of the nineteenth century has unquestionably been Russian. A number of years ago the *Saturday Review of Literature* reported the evaluations of John Galsworthy and Arnold Bennett: according to one of these eminent literati, of the twelve greatest novels written in the nineteenth century ten were Russian; according to the other, Russian literature was unquestionably the greatest in the nineteenth century.

Even granting that these judgments by two eminent English writers may be somewhat overstressed, it can scarcely be questioned that Russian literature reached unrivaled heights during the period considered. The names of Pushkin, Gogol, Lermontov, Gontcharov, Tolstoi, Dostoevski, Turgenev, to mention but a few of them, make the Russian literature of the last three quarters of the nineteenth century peerless.

This pre-eminence of Russian literature continued in the prerevolutionary twentieth century, with such novelists as A. Chekhov, M. Gorki, L. Andreev, I. Bunin, and many others, and such poets as Balmont, Briussov, Blok, Gumilev, and many others in the forefront. And with the close of the destructive phase of the Revolution, Russian literature gave definite signs of continuing this great prerevolutionary tradition. Though in no way equal to the Russian literature of the Pushkin-Gogol-Tolstoi-Dostoevski-Turgenev period, contemporary Russian literature is certainly second to none of the present period.

A similar "miracle" we observe in the field of *music*. Like Russian literature it suddenly emerges, bursts into a magnificent flowering, and at the end of the nineteenth century and during the twentieth century ripens into music that can certainly not be excelled anywhere in the world for that period. The rostrum of the nineteenth century includes Glinka, Tschaikovski, Mussorgsky, Rimski-Korsakov, Borodin, Dargomyzhski, Balakirev, and many others, not to mention the distinguished composers of a remarkable religious music that characterized the period. Stravinski, Prokoffiev, Shostakovitch, Scriabin, Rachmaninov, and many others — all of smaller stature than their predecessors — maintain the leadership today, during a century in which the composers of all nations occupy a lesser position than their predecessors. One manifestation of the extent to which musical culture had developed in prerevolutionary Russia is the fact that the greatest virtuoso musicians known in the United States, like Chaliapin, Heifetz, Piatigorski, Rachmaninov (as a pianist), and among the conductors Koussevitzki, to mention but a few names, were all born, reared, and trained in Russia.

The same story of a sudden creative explosion is told by Russian *drama, opera, theater, and ballet.* Prerevolutionary Russian opera was hardly rivaled anywhere; the same was true of the Russian ballet and theater, insofar as new creative forms are concerned. The Moscow Art Theater, the Imperial theaters in St. Petersburg and Moscow, the theaters of Madame Komissarjevski and others, set the highest of standards for this art during the nineteenth and twentieth centuries. Nearly every one associates the ballet first of all and most of all with Russia. This pre-eminence is due not only to the technique of the performance but also to the operas and plays created by the Russian authors. Only Germany with its Wagnerian opera excelled Russia up to the end of the nineteenth century. After that there was nothing truly great created by German genius in this field.

In a little less degree a similar renaissance of *painting* took place in Russia at the end of the nineteenth century and in the prerevolutionary twentieth century. A series of remarkable schools of painting, with extraordinarily brilliant artists, suddenly emerged on the Russian scene. Ryepin, Vasnetzov, Nesterov, Serov, Vrubel, Roerich, Petrov-Vodkin, Kustodiev, Maliavin, and many others put this art on a level unexcelled for the period by any country.

To sum up: we see in all fields of culture a sudden and most remarkable burst of cultural creativeness in Russia during the period being considered. In all of these fields Russia ceases to lag behind other nations and becomes their peer. Indeed, in certain fields it goes further and creates values greater than those of any other country.

Such a sudden burst of cultural creativeness is a rare phenomenon in history. Each great nation has its own hour for it. In most of the great nations it is rarely repeated. The period that begins in the second half of the nineteenth century was and is the historical "hour" of Russia. The creative genius of mankind, shifting in the course of time from nation to nation, found its chief dwelling place during this period in Russia (and the United States). In no other countries can one find a comparable cultural flowering during the period being considered. The naïveté and crass ignorance of those persons and nations that persist in regarding Russia as a backward country, as a poor and uncultured relative of the "civilized nations" and one which is not welcome in their "drawing rooms," must be apparent to anyone. Russia herself is hardly interested in visiting the "polished salons" of some of these civilized nations which lack every vestige of creative genius. It is not Russia, but rather these "polished sterilities," that would show to disadvantage if Russia did condescend to visit their salons. The deprecatory opinions of such countries are a matter of utter indifference to Russia.

6. *The Unique Progress of the United States*

Even more spectacular has been the sociocultural growth of the United States throughout its comparatively short history, and especially after the Civil War, the date coinciding significantly with the great reforms of 1861 and subsequent years in Russia. The story of this growth can be briefly outlined.

Vitally, through natural growth of the population and through immigration this nation has grown from a very moderate size to some 130 millions. The natural rate of growth of the population has been slower here than in Russia. Nevertheless up until the last two decades it was quite sufficient to maintain a growing population. In the last two decades, side by side with a notable decrease in the death rate, there has been a drop in the birth rate comparable to the trend in most of the industrialized Western countries. If, however, this decrease can be arrested, the nation will be able to escape the dangers of depopulation and to maintain its present population for an indefinite length of time. A much better course, however, would be to raise the birth rate without raising the death rate.

Otherwise, from the standpoint of health, the American population is as vigorous and healthy as any. Due to excellent living conditions its average expectation of life is longer than that of any other great nation in the world. All in all, in this field there has been an enormous improvement without any serious danger signals appearing as yet. Such dangers will be avoided much more surely if the currently fashionable low birth rate can be kept from falling any further.

Economically and *technologically* the nation climbed to an unprecedented level and occupied the first place among all the nations of the world. This is true by any criterion that we may choose: standard of living; average per capita income; total national wealth; industrial output; or, number of inventions and applied devices made since the 1870's. In all these respects the United States holds first place in the world. This record is unique indeed considering the shortness of time in which it has been achieved. In these technological and economic fields the creativeness of the American nation has been unsurpassed.

Among the many aspects of economic and technological progress in this country there is one specific aspect that deserves mention, namely the successful effort to secure for everybody a decent minimum of the necessities and material comforts of life. To be sure the success has not been absolute but from a comparative standpoint it has been more successful than any other attempt so far made. What is still hoped for in other countries is already achieved, to a great extent, in this country. Even its unemployed persons in recent years had a standard of living about as good as that of the employed laboring classes in a good many countries. The achievement is still more remarkable in that it was made peacefully, without practically any serious bloodshed or revolution attending it.

Sociopolitically the nation freed itself from the blot of *slavery* which marred its otherwise marvelous sociopolitical structure. Beginning as a small state it grew into the great empire that it is today — as powerful as any, and possibly even more powerful and influential than any. This growth has been achieved without any important sacrifice of its citizens' freedom, without any significant autocracy or absolutism in its government, without any notable loss of the privileges and rights of its citizens, and without any curtailment of equality of opportunity or any of the other values implied in the term democracy. Its sociopolitical regime still remains a government of the people, by the people, and for the people to a greater degree than in any other great empire.

Even its "imperialistic" expansion has been, as we have seen, more peaceful and just than that of most previous or contemporary great empires. All this is significant because in nearly every case known to history a nation that has grown from a small state into one of the greatest of empires, has done so at the cost of the freedoms and privileges of ordinary men and women. The United States has been able to grow without having to pay this terrible price.

One of the noteworthy merits of the American sociopolitical structure is the extraordinary role which *private individuals and associations* play in all fields of social and cultural life. In most other countries, with the exception of England, the position of the central government with respect to private association is incomparably greater than in the United States. Here with the natural exception of war time, private associations and societies carry on many more social and cultural functions — in education, business, fine arts, science, religion, law and ethics, recreation, and even politics — than the Federal and State governments. As the very nature of private association is voluntary co-operation, free from the coercion implicitly present in any government, this extraordinary development of private initiative, co-operation, and association is a sure sign of the real extent of freedom, voluntary association, and spontaneous sociality in the American nation — something that can hardly be matched by countries which have a strong central government. The relatively brief history of the establishment and development of sociopolitical structure in the United States has been one of the noblest and most successful experiments in the field.

Educationally, the country again made such a remarkable record that it is at the present time at the very top of all nations in this field. In spite of the huge influx of illiterate immigrants from other countries the United States has been able to achieve practically one hundred per cent literacy. Its system of elementary and secondary schools — private and public — is the most highly developed and the best equipped in the world. The same is true of its colleges, universities, and institutions of higher learning. Especially great has been the progress in all these institutions since the end of the nineteenth century and during the twentieth century. When to all this is added the role of adult education, of the press and radio, of numerous private organizations, and of the innumerable public lectures and addresses, the result is a degree of general education that is truly astounding. Not a small advantage in this whole educational system is the extraordinarily great role played by private schools, institutions, colleges, universities, academies, learned societies, and so on. It gives to the total educational system of this country an enormous diversity, as well as a much greater freedom from "one-track governmentally approved direction." It secures more than anything else a true freedom of thought, research, and education. It permits a genuine competition for success and survival among different and opposite theories, ideologies, and cultural values in marked contrast to a system of governmentally approved monopolistic values that exist and dominate for some time through an artificial elimination of all their competitors. If competition is necessary in the field of business to avoid economic stagnation and the domination of inferior goods or inferior economic systems and firms, it is still more urgent in the field of cultural values. Without it a nation is liable to become — intellectually, morally, artistically, and socially — an ossified intellectual mummy or a stagnant intellectual sterility.

Equipped with such an excellent educational apparatus the nation has made gigantic progress in the fields of *natural science and technology.* This has been so great that today in these fields it occupies the first place in the world. In the total number of scientific discoveries and technological inventions made throughout the world during the twentieth century the share of the United States has been larger than that of any other country. This leadership is likely to be retained for a long time to come.

Not so unique, but nevertheless considerable, has been the progress of the United States in the fields of *philosophy, the humanistic and social sciences, ethical and juridical disciplines, and in the field of the fine arts.* In these fields with the possible exception of architecture and applied art the United States can hardly be accorded first place among the nations of the world; nevertheless it has created, since the second part of the nineteenth century, a great literature, a number of important philosophical and ethical systems; well developed humanistic and social sciences; and significant values in painting, sculpture, drama, music, and especially architecture. In architecture the United States is at present the foremost country of the world. It also has the finest symphonic orchestras that are to be found in the world and in certain other technical aspects of music is outstanding. Its prospects for further development in these fields are even more promising.

This brief catalogue shows convincingly the truly unique record of sociocultural creativeness in the United States for the last century or so. If not from the standpoint of distance traversed, then surely in the magnitude of actual results achieved, the record of this nation exceeds even that of Russia. Both countries have developed their creative potentialities to a degree unparalleled by other nations during the period being considered. Put in another way, we can say that during the last one hundred years these two nations have truly experienced their "historical hour." They have thus not only come of age but have become the chief bearers of the torch of sociocultural creativeness. Herein lies an additional and very important similarity between the two nations.

7. *Implications of These Similarities for an Unbroken Peace*

The preceding chapters have demonstrated that far from being polar antitheses to each other, the two nations reveal a series of most striking similarities, geopolitically, psychologically, culturally, and socially. These similarities make the United States and Russia congenial to one another in many respects. The Russian and American people can understand one another much more easily than either of them can understand a good many other nations. Insofar as sociocultural similarities conduce toward peaceful relations between communities of men, the basic congeniality that exists between the fundamental values of the Russian and American people in large measure accounts for the long unbroken peace that has prevailed between these two nations. During some one hundred and sixty years of American history there has been a succession of the very different presidents, cabinet ministers, members of Congress and political parties, all of which had different interests, temperaments, likes and dislikes, ideologies, and what not. During the same period in Russia, czars and ruling groups with different psychologies, mental make-up, temperaments, preferences, and antipathies have succeeded one another. And yet, throughout this entire variegated pageant a continuous peace has been maintained between the two nations. This means that war and peace depend very little upon the personal fancies and whims, preferences and dislikes of this or that ruler, or upon whether he is autocratic or democratic. They depend rather upon the factors that we have been stressing in this work. Inasmuch as these factors have been present in the relationships between the United States and Russia they are responsible for the existence of unbroken peaceful relations between the two nations. As these two factors continue to exist at the present time and will doubtless continue to exist in the near future, they are bound to perpetuate this noble record of peace between the two nations, regardless of the personal whims of their rulers. If and when these rulers become unwise and begin to commit one blunder after another, there may conceivably arise some temporary differences and quarrels between the countries. But even these conflicts are bound to be minor and can hardly lead to an armed conflict. The total configuration of sociocultural forces is fortunately loaded against such a tragedy.

CHAPTER EIGHT

MUTUAL INFLUENCE OF THE TWO NATIONS UPON EACH OTHER'S SOCIOCULTURAL LIFE

1. *Influence of the United States Upon Russia*

It is inevitable that two such nations as Russia and the United States, whose basic values are so congenial and whose dealings with one another have always been peaceful, should exert a considerable influence upon each other's social and cultural life. The relationship between these two countries has indeed been no mere vacuous compatibility but has entailed a dynamic and creatively fruitful influence upon one another. The mentality, social life, and culture of each have been fertilized and enriched by that of the other nation, to the benefit of each. The real magnitude of this social and cultural impact has hardly been appreciated by most persons.

The influence of the United States upon Russia began long ago and directly or indirectly introduced into Russia a vast assortment of American values, making them an organic part of Russian culture and thereby tangibly shaping Russian life and society. The principal fields in which American influence has been particularly strong are: first, the field of sociopolitical organization; second, the field of technology and business; third, the field of literature, architecture, cinema, science, and philosophy; fourth, the general mentality of the Russian people.

The impact of the United States upon the sociopolitical life of Russia has been due not so much to any active or deliberate effort on the part of this country, as to the *"catalytic effects"* of the very existence of America's system of sociopolitical organization. Most people, including social scientists, do not realize that in social life the mere existence of two agents side by side will involve some degree of influence by one upon the other. A comparable process is that which chemists call "catalysis." The process involves the acceleration in a chemical reaction that is produced by the mere presence of a catalytic agent which itself appears to remain unchanged and non-participating throughout the reaction. In social life the mere association or coexistence of two persons calls forth some kind of emotion, whether it be rage or love or hatred. Likewise the mere existence of a certain society exerts upon another society some tangible influence which is generally far more effective than any that the propagandist is able to exert. If during the last two decades Communism or Fascism has affected most of the world in some degree, these effects are to be attributed not so much to any deliberate proselytism by its government as to the mere fact of their existence as political entities, or, expressed, otherwise, to their catalytic influence. This catalytic influence has been infinitely greater than that of all the Communist or Fascist propagandists taken together.

Similarly *the very fact of the emergence and existence of the United States, with its political constitution and organization, has continuously influenced Russian political thought and political activities.* This influence began as early as the reign of Czar Alexander I who, following the victory over Napoleon's invading armies, sought to establish a liberal federation of European nations upon principles somewhat similar to those of the American Constitution. Unfortunately the Czar's liberal plans were opposed by Metternich and some of the European powers and its only fruition was the Holy Alliance.[1]

America provided similar inspiration to the leaders of

[1] Even earlier. Already in 1789 Benj. Franklin was elected an honorary member of Russian Academy of Sciences. In the works of the leaders of political thought of the eighteenth century, Radyscev and Novikov, (1784) we find the highest praise of the United States and G. Washington. Since that time this praise became traditional in Russian social thought and literature.

Russia's first revolutionary movement in the nineteenth century, the *Decembrist Revolution* of 1825. One of the members of this uprising, Colonel Muraviev, had worked out a plan for the reorganization of Russia along federal lines, patterned after the United States Constitution in many respects. His constitution was formally approved by the Northern Society of the Decembrists. Since that time, the political organization and activities of the United States have been studied, and discussed in university courses, by students of politics, by popular journals and newspapers and by leading statesmen of Russia. Above all they have been genuinely admired and some of their elements have been borrowed and introduced into various sociopolitical institutions of Russia. The idea of a people's democracy has meant in Russia first of all and most of all the American political organization. Some traits of the American Constitution, such as the principle of the separation and balance of the executive, legislative, and judicial functions; such as the independence and high standards of the United States Supreme Court; not to mention the very idea of a government of the people, by the people, and for the people; have been especially appreciated in Russia, and many attempts have been made to incorporate them into Russian political organization and activities. The same is true of the exceptionally great role played in the United States by private initiative and by private associations and organizations. Suffering from overcentralization and from the unduly great role played by government in Russia and the excessively modest role played by private organizations, Russia has a real need for these components of American sociopolitical organization and activities. Hence their popularity in Russia. This explains why the recent blueprints of the new Russian Constitution, drawn up under the Kerenski regime, were so heavily influenced by the American Constitution and why it intentionally planned to introduce many of its features. Even the new Soviet Constitution of 1936 as it exists on paper bears many traits taken from the American Constitution. Similarly, when the time comes to tailor a new constitution for a postwar Russia adapted to normal conditions there is hardly any doubt that many of these features of the American Constitution will be successfully incorporated into the new constitution.

The magnitude of the impact that *American technology and business organization* has made upon Russian technology and economic life is something that needs no arguing. It is a well known fact. First of all, the United States has *indirectly* exerted a profound influence through Russia's adoption of more and more American inventions, ranging from the steamboat, agricultural machines, electrical devices, and the telephone, up to the automobile, and mass production technology in industry. Indirectly then the United States has notably shaped the economic and technological life of Russia just as it has moulded that of all other countries.

Besides this indirect influence, this nation has affected Russian technological and economic life *directly* in many ways. Thus, American engineers and business experts have been called to advise and to guide the construction or reconstruction of this or that technological and economic enterprise. Such invitations occurred before the Revolution and assumed an enormous scale during the revolutionary reconstruction of Russia. Every one knows that American experts played the decisive role in the reindustrialization and economic reorganization of Russia. The greatest construction feats of that period, like the Dnieprostroi and Magnitogorsk projects, as well as the development of great new industrial centers, were made under the direct planning, advice, and guidance of American experts. An American Colonel Hugh L. Cooper, builder of the Dnieper Dam, was the first foreigner to be decorated by the Supreme Soviet of the U. S. S. R. Practically all the main branches of industry in the Soviet Union have been remodeled and shaped under the guidance of American experts.

Another form of this direct influence has been the training of Russian experts, engineers, and business managers in the United States. This again occurred not only in the period of revolutionary reconstruction but also before it. For instance, Mr. Khilkov, who became minister of transportation in Russia and occupied this post for several years and who was instrumental in the development of Russia's railway system, spent several years in the United States studying American railroad systems both theoretically and practically, by becoming an employee of certain American railroads, beginning with the lowest rank and passing subsequently to higher ranks. His case is not unique. Scores of Russians stayed in this country and studied various branches of industry and afterwards applied their experience in their homeland. This training of prospective Russian experts in the United States assumed a very large scale during the revolutionary reconstruction. Hundreds and hundreds of Russians have been sent to this country by the Soviet Government, aided by the generous help of many American technological institutes and engineering and economic departments of American universities. Large industrial firms of this country, such as General Electric, the Ford Company, General Motors, and so on, have been and are training Russian specialists in the fields of technology and business management. Having returned to Russia they have become its technological and business leaders. The influence exerted in this way has indeed been enormous. Even a casual visitor in Russia is able to see that the whole industrial and technical plant has been remodeled along strictly American patterns, so closely in fact that the buildings and fixtures themselves seem to be a second edition of American forms. Russian experts who have never been abroad have systematically studied, both before and after the Revolution, every new American invention, device, and method that appeared in their fields. Many American machines and gadgets reaching Russia have been copied and reproduced there. When these and other manifestations of the impact made by the United States upon Russian technology and industry are kept in mind, one can readily understand why the terms: "industrialization," and "Americanization," "technology," "efficiency," "inventiveness" and "Americanism" have often been used in Russia as synonyms. One can also understand why the highest ideal of Russia's industrial development has been to reach the American level of achievement. No other country, certainly not within the last few decades, has exerted so great an influence upon Russia in these fields of social endeavor. The industrialization and reindustrialization of Russia has indeed been largely a process of "Americanization."

While this fact is about as well known here as it is in Russia, much less is known of *the cultural influence that American literature, and recently architecture and movies, has exerted upon Russian culture.* Nevertheless this influence has been very considerable. Spiritual congeniality between the two nations is responsible for the extensive diffusion and popularity of American literature in Russia. There is hardly any classic of American literature that has not been translated into Russian and met with as warm a reception as it did in this country. All the main works of Fenimore Cooper, Mark Twain, Longfellow, Edgar Allan Poe, Melville, Walt Whitman, Jack London, O. Henry, Harriet Beecher Stowe, Hawthorne, and more recently those of Sinclair Lewis, Upton Sinclair, Theodore Dreiser, John Steinbeck, to mention but a few, were translated and widely read in Russia long before the Revolution and after it. Some of these works like *Uncle Tom's Cabin,* the *Prince and the Pauper, Tom Sawyer, The Adventures of Huckleberry Finn, Hiawatha, The Raven,* and some of the mysteries by Poe, as well as many stories of Jack London, have been possibly even more popular in Russia than they were in this country. Some of these have become the highly popular "must" readings of Russian children.

Modern reinforced-concrete *architectural styles* as developed in America have, in a modified version, become the dominant architecture of modern Russia.

American *movies* likewise have enjoyed an extraordinary popularity in Russia both before and after the Revolution.

Finally, American *science,* both natural and social — and even American *philosophy* — had entered the cultural life of Russia before the Revolution and continued this penetration afterwards in ever increasing degree. American natural sciences and technology have been studied in Russia most carefully. Every important theory or discovery has received the attention and consideration that it deserves. American scientific publications could be found, except during the destructive years of the Revolution, in any university and in all the main libraries of the country. Generally speaking, throughout the twentieth century American natural science has exerted as powerful an influence upon the natural sciences of Russia as have those of any other country, and this influence is increasing steadily.

The same is true of the *social sciences, particularly of sociology.* The works of such American sociologists as Lester Ward and Franklin Giddings have been translated into Russian and have become required works for the scholars in this field.

In the field of *psychology and philosophy* the works of William James and later on of W. McDougall were translated into Russian and in my student days were used as some of the basic texts in several Russian universities — especially James' *Psychology, Pragmatism,* and *Varieties of Religious Experience,* and McDougall's *Social Psychology.*

Moreover, American symphonic *music* (of Harris, Copeland, and others) as well as American jazz and swing have recently made considerable inroad into Russian music. Symphonic American music is frequently performed but jazz and swing so far have not met with the same success that they have had in this and certain other countries.

Finally, the *English language* was one of the three main foreign languages, along with German and French, that were required and taught before the Revolution in high schools and universities. With World War I, the German language ceased to be compulsory and English became one of the two required foreign languages. At the present time English is accorded primary importance among the foreign languages taught and studied in Russia.

The last but by no means least influence that the United States has exerted has been upon the *psychology, mentality, and conduct of the Russian people.* The net result of this influence can be summed up in a short but weighty formula: *The United States, Americans, and Americanism have for a long time been exceedingly popular in Russia.* Many specific values as well as the total value-system of this nation are tremendously admired, deeply appreciated, often imitated, in part absorbed, and not infrequently looked upon as an ideal by the rank and file of the Russian population.

Whenever there appears among Russians an unusually energetic, efficient, inventive, and optimistic type of person he is often nicknamed "our Russian American." Tasks that are well executed are referred to as "done in the American way." Any manifestation of fair play is likewise characterized as "the American spirit." Every step forward in the field of technology and business administration as well as in the field of social service, democracy, and justice, is again regarded as a step towards "Americanism." In the same way Russians admire the lucky combination of idealism with practical realism; of practical generosity and kindness joined with shrewdness and hardheadedness, of liberty combined with orderliness and lawfulness; and the indomitable energy, perseverance, and unwillingness to admit defeat, whether in a struggle with nature or with adverse social conditions. Facts and phenomena of that kind are regarded as typically American. These examples give an idea of how Americans and

American values are regarded in Russia and why they are so greatly admired. If a plain Russian is asked with what country Russia should be most closely united, the answer, in an enormous majority of cases, will be, "America," meaning by it the United States. "America" has become a symbol of all these and many other positive values. In a certain sense it has become a living legend, an incarnation of the things hoped and aspired for. Sometimes this idealization of the United States goes even beyond the real virtues of this nation.

Such an attitude toward the United States is not only typical but is highly important for both countries and for their present and future relationship. It indicates not only the favorable impression made by "America" upon the Russian nation, but it is the best and most solid foundation for a further fruitful co-operation between the two countries. It is one of the two main forces that make possible such a co-operation. It also evidences — and very well — the congeniality of the souls and cultures of the two peoples.

2. *Influence of Russia Upon the United States*

Very considerable too has been the impact of Russia upon the United States and its culture. This influence has been most noticeable in the sociopolitical and scientific fields and especially in those of literature, music, and the theater. It has been both direct and indirect, and has been growing as a whole throughout the period of contact between the two countries.

In the *sociopolitical field* Russia has influenced the destiny of this nation through the help it has lent on a number of crucial occasions, particularly when this nation was comparatively small, or when it was in a state of acute crisis such as that of the Civil War. The consistently friendly attitude of Russia during these critical periods of American history played a very tangible role in shaping the sociopolitical history of this country.

More directly, through the catalytic factor of the emergence and existence of the Soviet regime, Russia has exerted and is exerting a tremendous impact upon the United States, regardless of whether it is positive or negative. The magnitude of this catalytic influence far exceeds any that may emanate from the organized propaganda of Russian Communists or their American sympathizers. The Soviet system, established in Russia, has been the most radical political experiment of recent times, and as such it has exerted far greater influence upon the political life of this globe than any other sociopolitical innovation of the twentieth century. In common with other countries the United States has not escaped this impact. The influence has manifested itself not only in the appearance of a Communist party in this country — by itself this is a small and negligible matter — but in the fact of the Soviet system's entering the mind of the people, penetrating the political thought of both the high-brow and the man in the street, and working into practically every compartment of American sociocultural life. Regardless as to whether people are friendly or inimical to the Soviet system of sociopolitical organization, they all — friends and foes — have to reckon and deal with it. In this sense the Soviet system has become an inherent component of the sociopolitical thinking and activity of modern times. In this meaning the real impact that the Russian experiment has exerted upon these fields must be apparent. One can hardly open any current newspaper, or a copy of any magazine, or any recent book in political science, sociology, economics, social ethics, or philosophy without finding a great deal of space devoted to this subject. One can hardly attend any important political rally or any serious college course in the social sciences without hearing something said of the Soviet system. It forms a topic for discussion in congressional sessions, for church sermons, for public lectures, and for everyday chatting among friends and neighbors. Hundreds of volumes have been devoted to the subject, not to mention the avalanche of Communistic publications. What is still more important, every discussion of the topic is usually carried on with the most intense emotionality — by its proponents as well as its opponents and enemies. Dozens of special committees of which the Dies Congressional Committee is but one, have been organized for the propagation or repression of the Soviet system.

The impact of the Soviet system of sociopolitical organization has not been confined to mere discussion. It has exerted a most powerful influence upon the actual course of sociopolitical life and activities of the leading statesmen as well as those of the rank and file of people. Even more, owing to the inevitable expansion of governmental regulation and control [2] which is the necessary corollary to depression and war, the very organization of government, in this as in other countries, has undergone a change in the direction of the Soviet system. In this shift several traits of the Soviet system have been intentionally copied and borrowed.

Thus, for good or for ill, Russia has exerted and is exerting a very profound influence upon our sociopolitical life.

Just as American science has influenced Russian science, so a reverse influence has been operating. *Directly and indirectly Russian science, through its contributions, has*

---

[2] The main factor in the expansion of governmental regimentation and control has always been the appearance of social emergency, such as famine, war, revolution, pestilence, and the like. The disappearance or decline of social emergency and calamity have also regularly led to a decline of governmental regimentation and control. The Soviet system emerged during one of the greatest emergencies in the history of Russia — a great war, a revolution, and their satellites famine and pestilence. For this reason the present war has led to an enormous increase of governmental regimentation in all the belligerent countries. So far as an almost unlimited and centralized regimentation of government is the heart of the Soviet system, a shift in this direction in all the belligerent countries is a shift towards the Soviet system. See about this law in my *Man and Society in Calamity* (E. P. Dutton & Company, New York, 1942), chap. vii.

markedly influenced American science: natural, humanistic, and social. Important discoveries of Russian natural scientists, such as those of Lobachevski and the brilliant school of Russian mathematicians; of Mendelyeev and other eminent Russian chemists; of Setchenov and other biologists; and of I.Pavlov and a host of Russian physiologists and psychologists; these discoveries have significantly affected the natural sciences of this country. This reciprocal influence between the natural sciences of both countries has continued with increasing effectiveness to the present time.

The same is true of the mutual influence of the social and humanistic sciences. Russian social and historical sciences have influenced the corresponding disciplines in the United States through many channels. One such channel has been through the works of Communist theorizers, like Lenin, Trotski, Stalin, Bukharin, and many others, translated, published, and widely circulated in this country. Another channel was the publication in most of the principal European languages of the important works of various Russian social scientists and social philosophers, such as the great theorizer of law, L. Petrajitzki; great Russian historians like Klutchevski, and lesser ones like Milyukov, Platonov, Kornilov; the works of notable social and general philosophers like N. Berdiaiev, N. Losski, V. Soloviev; and so on. A third channel has been through the works of Russian scholars who subsequently became American citizens and professors. These scholars, who number in their ranks a good many eminent social scientists such as M. Rostovtzev and others, have introduced into American social science new values deriving from their Russian heritage. Through these and similar channels Russian science in all its branches has entered the scientific culture of this nation.

But especially great has been the influence of *Russian literature, music, and drama* upon the American mind and culture. Great Russian writers have, in the first place, influenced American writers in their manner of composition. Being translated into English the works of the writers became a very important element in the literature and culture of this nation. The works of Tolstoi and Dostoevski, of Turgenev and Gogol, of A. Chekhov and Gorki, on up to the recent works of the Soviet writers, have become known to most of the really cultured persons in this country. Some of them have even turned into best sellers for the public at large, such as the recent edition of Tolstoi's *War and Peace*. English literature excepted, the literature of Russia has probably been read and become known in this country better than that of any other foreign country. It has entered American culture as an organic component.

The same is true of *Russian music,* particularly symphonic music. A recent investigation into the frequency with which the works of various composers have appeared in the repertoire of the eight main American orchestras from 1876 to 1940[3] shows that Tchaikovski has occupied either third or fourth place among all the composers, being exceeded only by Beethoven, and for some of the years in that period by Wagner, Brahms, Mozart and Bach, while for other years he exceeded all these except Beethoven. Next to the works of these truly great composers of all time, among the composers of modern period so far as frequency of playing is concerned, rank the compositions of such notable Russians as Glinka, Rimski-Korsakov, Mussorgsky, Stravinski, Prokoffieff, Miaskovski, Shostakovitch, Scriabin, Rachmaninov, Glazunov, Gliere, Rubinstein, Borodin, Liadov, Balakirev, Molotov, Dukelski, Beresovski, Ippolitov-Ivanov, and others. While due to Beethoven, Bach, and Mozart the German-Austrian music has occupied the first place in the repertoire of the main American orchestras, the music of Russia has had the second place. If we take the composers of the twentieth century, Russian

[3] J. H. Mueller and K. Hevner. *Trends in Musical Taste* (Bloomington, 1943).

music is accorded first place in the repertoire of the eight main American orchestras. Russian folk music has also become highly popular in America and is now really an inherent part of it. Tunes like the *Volga Boatman, Dark Eyes,* and hundreds of other Russian folk songs have been popularized to an extraordinary extent by numerous bands and singers.

Moreover, it is enough to take the ranking virtuoso musicians of this country — violinists, cellists, pianists, and others, including conductors (Heifetz, Piatigorski, Rachmaninov, Koussevitzki, and so on) — as well as the members of the leading orchestras to see that Russia has exerted a great influence upon American musical culture. The proportion of such musicians trained in Russia and with a Russian background is very considerable among leading musicians of this country. In these and similar ways the influence of Russia upon American music has been enormous.

Very pregnant too has been the influence of the *Russian theater,* particularly opera, drama, comedy, tragedy, and ballet, upon the American theater and ballet. Besides staging a considerable number of Russian plays, operas, and ballets, American theatrical art has definitely borrowed from and imitated that of Russia, whether it be the art of the Russian opera, or that of the drama, such as the Moscow Art Theater, or that of the Russian ballet which is still dominantly Russian even in its personnel in this country. Even American movies have not been entirely exempt from this Russian theatrical influence.

To sum up: in the fields that we have surveyed, Russia has greatly contributed to American culture, to its diversification, enrichment, and ennoblement. Each of the two cultures has notably enriched the other; each has given the other a series of true and magnificent values that have become an organic part of the life and culture of the two nations. Instead of interchanging blows and bullets, destruction and hatred, the two nations have freely and generously given to each other the best of what they have created. The intensity and magnitude of this blessed exchange testifies again to the deep congeniality of the souls and cultures of the two nations.

With this we may conclude our discussion of the profound and important similarities in the mentality, social institutions, and culture of the two nations. This similarity, together with the lack of irreconcilable conflicts among their vital values, has been the decisive factor in their long and unbroken peace. The same considerations presage a continuation of their creative co-operation in the future for the mutual benefit of both nations, as well as that of mankind. There still remains, however, one problem that seems to contradict this diagnosis, namely the problem of Russian Communism, Sovietism, and Revolution, which evidently cannot be reconciled with the American way of life and system of values. The problem is so important that it cannot be either dodged or passed by. Therefore I shall discuss it in the next chapter.

CHAPTER NINE

THE RUSSIA OF THE POST-DESTRUCTIVE PHASE OF THE REVOLUTION

1. *The Ghosts of Communism and Capitalism*

If Russia were still purely communistic and the United States were still purely capitalistic; if the Russia of today were the Russia of the first period of the Revolution (especially of the years 1918-1922), and the United States were in the same position as in the years 1920-1929 (before the Great Depression), then obviously an irreconcilable conflict between the two nations would have been inevitable. No lasting reconciliation of these diametrically opposed systems of values would have been possible; therefore any real and durable co-operation would have been excluded. If the present situation were indeed such, those who voice the inevitability of the conflict between Russia and this country, entertaining strong suspicions and intense apprehensions respecting Russian Communism, and advocating our either undertaking a crusade against Communistic Russia or else holding aloof from her as far as possible, would have been quite right.

Fortunately their premises, as well as the conclusions built upon these premises, are entirely erroneous. They seem to have been asleep for at least the last fifteen years and to have failed to notice the profound changes that have occurred in both countries during that period. They have failed to observe that the classic capitalist system, based upon the classic theory of private property as something to possess, use, manage, and dispose of without any restrictions, has been dying out in the United States during the last fifty years, and especially during the last fifteen years, having been replaced in greater part by the system of "corporate economy" or "governmentally managed economy," both of which are fundamentally different from the classic system of capitalism and private property.

They were even more obtuse in overlooking the fact that by the middle of the thirties the Communist phase of the Russian Revolution, with its militant atheism, its wholesale rejection of "bourgeois values," its cruelty and bestiality, its fanatical ideology, and so on, was virtually at an end and that Russia was gradually entering the post-revolutionary stage — that of reconstructing its shattered household in conformity with the vital national trends disrupted by the first phase of the Revolution. They do not realize that American Capitalism and Russian Communism are now little more than the ghosts of their former selves. In discussing their inevitable conflict they are actually talking of the struggle of corpses — something which occurs only in the realm of nightmares or pathological phantasmagoria. Let us look more closely at what has happened to the Russian Revolution and to Communism during the last two decades or so, in order to free ourselves from these illusions.

2. The Cycle of Major Revolutions

Practically all thoughtful investigators of major revolutions — including, more recently, Alexis de Tocqueville and H. Taine — have correctly observed that they succeed in destroying permanently only those institutions and trends which were already moribund and which would have died out even in the absence of any revolution. Those which are vital are only temporarily disrupted by the destructive phase of the revolution. With the passing of this phase they re-emerge, resuming their prerevolutionary course *pari passu* with the decline of the revolution and especially of its disintegration.[1]

3. *The Cycle of the Russian Revolution*

This generalization holds good for the Russian Revolution. In the period of roughly 1918 to 1934 it eliminated all the decadent institutions and cultural values of Russia. Temporarily it undermined also most of the creative institutions and disrupted vital prerevolutionary trends. To an observer unacquainted with the actual course of the Revolution, the situation looked like the abrupt termination of a long era of Russian history and national culture and the sudden emergence of an entirely different sociocultural order. Indeed, this is precisely how the work of the Revolution has been characterized by its leaders and victims, as well as by a host of superficial observers. As a matter of fact, however, its destructive phase was ended around the middle of the thirties. Thereafter the course of Russian sociocultural life made a sharp turn and assumed quite a different character — one almost directly opposite to that of its earlier course. A great deal of what the Revolution had to destroy in its first period it now undertook to rebuild. Much of what it had once slandered it now extolled. Conversely, many pseudo values and institutions that it had created in its first stage it commenced to tear down in its second period. The vital sociocultural values temporarily submerged in the first phase of the Revolution have progressively reasserted themselves and have forced the Revolution to retreat more and more until it has very nearly

[1] See my *Sociology of Revolution* (J. P. Lippincott Co., 1925) and *Dynamics*, Vol. III.

liquidated itself. Such, in brief, is the cyclic formula of the Russian Revolution.

This course is the more striking in that Stalin is still the dictator of Russia and that Russia seems to be ruled by the same Communist party which presided over the destructive phase of the Revolution. To a superficial observer this con-- stitutes unimpeachable evidence of the unchanged character of the Revolution. In their heart of hearts the Communist leaders possibly still cherish the same aspirations and values that animated them in the first phase of the Revolution. Nevertheless, their secret aspirations are quite irrelevant to the actual course of events. What matters is the kind of activities which Stalin and the Communist party have been actually carrying on since the middle of the thirties. What is still more important is the nature and direction of the change which the sociocultural life of Russia has undergone during that period. When the problem is stated in this form, the only form scientifically and sociologically relevant, the answer is: first, Stalin and the Communist party during the second period of the Revolution have been performing a task not only different from, but to a considerable extent directly opposed to, what they did in its first phase. Second, the direction of sociocultural change in this later period is very different from, and partly opposite to, that of the earlier period. This radical volte-face was executed by the Soviet leaders under the pressure of irresistible sociocultural forces whose bidding they could not ignore save at the cost of being ousted from their position of power. They have subsequently been increasingly extolling much of what they had denounced before, and decrying many "gods of Communism" which they had earlier exalted. Otherwise they would have been overthrown long since, being replaced by leaders willing to obey the inexorable mandates of history. Such transformations of the leaders of revolutions have happened many times before.

4. *The Decline of Communism and the Growth of a Vital New Russia*

The facts that corroborate this conclusion are too numerous to be enumerated in full. Here are a few typical examples.

From the Destruction of the Family to Its Rebuilding. During the first stage of the Communist Revolution its leaders deliberately tried to destroy the monogamic family and marriage as the cornerstones of the system of capitalism and private property which they had undertaken to abolish. Complete liberty of divorce was accordingly introduced. Free love was glorified in terms of the famous analogy of "the glass of water": if a person is thirsty, it is immaterial with what glass he satisfies his thirst; if a person is sexually thirsty, it is equally unimportant with what "sexual glass his thirst is quenched." Moreover, the legal distinction between socially sanctioned marriage and casual sexual intercourse was practically abolished. The Communist law spoke of contracts between males and females for the satisfaction of their sexual needs. A contract could be for an indefinite period; for a definite period — say a year, a week, or a month; or for a single case. It is evident that under these conditions not only was there complete freedom of divorce, but the parties were not obliged to bother with formal divorce proceedings: a wife or husband could be divorced without being notified of the step. Neither were they required to register their "marriage." Polygamy, bigamy, and any other form of marriage were quite legitimate under these provisions. Abortions were welcomed, and even facilitated in state institutions.

The consequences of such "freedom" had already been pointed out by Aristotle in his criticism of Plato's system of communism as applied to women. Hordes of wild, homeless children soon became a real menace to the Soviet Union itself. Millions of lives were wrecked, especially those of girls and women. The Soviet law entitled a woman or girl to ali-

mony from the father of her children. According to some
foreign eulogists of Communism, this alimony amply protected the interests of the wife and children. In fact, however,
if the total income of the man was, say, twelve dollars a month
and it was factually on an average less than this, and if on
these twelve dollars he had to maintain himself, his first wife
and children, his second wife and her children, and so on, it
is obvious that his income could not possibly suffice to support
him and all his dependents. To cut a long and tragic story
short, it is enough to say that after several years of experimen-
tation even the Soviet Government and the Communist party
came to perceive the harmfulness of their policy. Under the
pressure of the catastrophic consequences of the experiment
they were forced to abandon the policy, step by step, and
finally to replace it with the opposite one — namely, that of
reconstructing the family and marriage on their prerevolutionary basis. The theory of the "glass of water" was repudi-
ated and its belated partisans came to be styled "counter-
revolutionists" and punished accordingly. It was replaced by
a rigorously Victorian code of faithfulness and loyalty for life,
by a glorification of sexual chastity and virginity akin to the
precepts of Saint Paul, and by a series of radical changes in
the laws governing marriage and the family. Liberty of divorce
was reduced to its prerevolutionary status. The difference
between socially sanctioned marriage and incidental sex relations was sharply emphasized. The sanctity of marriage was
reinstated. Abortions were penalized with the exception of
the few legitimate cases dictated either by the safety of the
life of the mother or by other reasons sanctioned by most
of the laws of the Western countries. In 1943 even co-
educational system was replaced by that of separate schools
for boys and girls in the high schools. In brief, in its post-
destructive period the Russian Revolution entirely reversed
its policy and was forced to restore marriage and the family
in about the same form as that in which they had existed

before the Revolution. By 1940 the cycle was about completed. At that time the family and marriage were more nearly "Victorian" (without the hypocritical traits of the Victorian family) than in most of the Western countries. "Free love" (in a specific sense) was less frequent in the Russia of 1940 than in many other lands. Such is the cycle passed through by the Russian family in the short period of twenty years. The Revolution, having attempted in vain to destroy it, finally yielded to the pressure of sociocultural forces too strong for it to ignore.

From the Persecution of Religion to Its Toleration. A similar cycle, not yet completed, is observable in the field of *religion and freedom of conscience.* We have seen (in Chapter Five) that the first period of the Revolution was marked by a negative or hostile attitude toward religion, particularly toward the Russian Orthodox Church. Religion was persecuted and eradicated by every means at the disposal of the Communist rulers. The coexistence of the Communist state and a religious system seemed to be impossible. After the beginning of the thirties a notable change became apparent in this field. The militant atheism of the Communist party began to decline, persecution slackened, and a certain amount of religious toleration appeared. Since that time this new policy has made notable progress, so that a fairly cordial co-operation now exists between the Soviet Government and the Russian Orthodox religion, the two organizations working side by side in the defense of the country as well as in several other fields of endeavor. Persecution and discrimination have largely disappeared. The value of religion is explicitly recognized. Great Russian religious leaders of the past are lauded by the government, especially for their services to the nation. Conversely, the attitude of the Russian Orthodox Church and its hierarchy toward the government is no longer as apprehensive and implicitly negative as it was during the period of the persecution. The Orthodox Church is entirely separate from the state; adherence to it is purely voluntary; it enjoys no privileges not accorded other religions; it is democratic and elective in its hierarchy; it retains the headship of the Patriarch, established by the All-Russian Orthodox Congress in 1917; the priests and bishops are no longer state bureaucrats, but chiefly charismatic spiritual and moral leaders. In brief, the Russian Orthodox Church has adopted the patterns clearly formulated by it before the Revolution.

Of course, it would be incorrect to state that complete religious freedom has been attained, or that the Church is fully independent of State Government. The Communist leaders have not radically changed their convictions: they would probably prefer to have either no church and no religion or else only such as would promote the realization of their objectives. Nevertheless, the position of religion and the Church in Russia is profoundly different from what it was in the first period of the Revolution. Although the cycle is not yet terminated, it has run two thirds of its course. There is no doubt that it will be completed, regardless of the personal attitude and convictions of the rulers and the dominant party. Religion, particularly the Russian Orthodox religion, has stood the crucial test of the Revolution and, despite the great diminution in the number of its adherents, it has emerged purified, spiritualized, and ennobled. The growth of its following is merely a matter of time.[2]

From Despotism to a Modicum of Freedom. To a less extent the same trend is observable in the case of *freedom of thought, speech, the press, and association.* In the first period the Communist dogma claimed that all these "freedoms" were but "hypocritical bourgeois prejudices." They were jeered at, denied, and rejected. In the second period the new Soviet Constitution of 1936 officially proclaimed them to be the inalienable rights of the citizens. So far this new principle has fallen short of complete fulfillment. There is still only the government press in Russia; all the printing establishments

[2] See N. S. Timashev, *Religion in Soviet Russia.* (Sheed, 1942)

are in the hands of the government; nothing can be published without the approval of the authorities; any fiery opposition speech is likely to land the speaker into jail; no association is permissible without the approval of the authorities; and so on. However, within the framework of the governmentally controlled press and thought much greater latitude now exists for dissenting opinions than during the first period of the Revolution. At present many theories and evaluations can be expressed and published without incurring imprisonment or other punishment. During the earlier period, only works directly or indirectly related to Communism and the Soviet Government were published and circulated. By 1940 a wide range of literary works (some including a sharp criticism of Communism and Sovietism and of the Communist leaders), large numbers of scientific, scholastic, and other works having no direct relationship to Communism, and even a few religious and philosophical works were being published in ever-increasing proportions at the expense of the dwindling volume of Communist literature. The general atmosphere was much more conducive to the growth of free and liberal thought than hitherto. In brief, freedom of thought, speech, and the press has been expanding in many ways during the second period of the Revolution. Though the progress achieved in this field is still very modest and the cycle is far from being completed, there is no doubt that the new trend will continue to develop. Here again Russia is reviving the trends that were under way before the Revolution.

From Vilification to Glorification of Russian Culture. Still more striking is the later attitude of the government toward general cultural values. During the destructive phase of the Revolution not only were religion, the family, and juridical and ethical values denied and vilified, but even the achievements of great Russian authors, composers, scientists, and philosophers were scathingly denounced. The foremost Russian writers, such as Pushkin, Tolstoy, and Dostoevski, were decried as "mouthpieces of the degenerate aristocracy." Several of their works, like Dostoevski's *The Possessed*, were placed on the *Index Librorum Prohibitorum;* even his *Brothers Karamazov* was banned on the stage of the Moscow Art Theater.

The same is true of musical compositions and composers. Several compositions of Tschaikovsky, like the *Marche Slave* and the *1812 Overture*, as well as several operas of Rimski-Korsakov, were debarred from public performance. The reason for these and similar prohibitions was, of course, the alleged need for suppressing the "counterrevolutionary spirit."

This negative attitude toward, and crass intolerance of, "bourgeois values" was rampant during that period. Thousands of books, often remote from the realm of politics, were ordered to be taken from the libraries and destroyed or else were withdrawn from circulation. Most non-Marxian historical and social-science works, and works on psychology and philosophy that deviated from the orthodox interpretation of Marxian dogma by Lenin, Trotsky, Bukharin, or Stalin, were placed in this class. An example of interest to the American public is the suppression of the works of William James (translated into Russian), which fell into the category of prohibited "counterrevolutionary" literature.

Likewise in the field of the fine arts generally, everything that deviated from the prescribed standard of the Communist Government was directly or indirectly debarred. For instance, in the early years of the Revolution the government was an enthusiastic proponent of various "futuristic" and "modernistic" styles. Therefore anything, no matter how incongruous, created in these styles was welcomed, and anything in the "antiquated bourgeois and counterrevolutionary style" was suppressed or disfavored.

This misguided zeal went so far that in the university and high school curriculums most of the social, humanistic, and philosophical disciplines that were not Marxian were abolished, being replaced by what was nicknamed "Communist Theology," consisting of an orthodox history of the Communist party, the Communist Revolution, the political constitution of the U.S.S.R., the economic organization of the Soviet Union, and a primer of Communist dogma. The non-Marxian professors were dismissed (if not shot or imprisoned). There was hardly any possibility of publishing a work in these fields if it did not conform strictly to the dogma of official truth as prescribed by governmental fiat.

Even the mathematical and natural sciences were declared to be "bourgeois," and an attempt was made to replace them with "proletarian" mathematics, physics, chemistry, and biology. The mostly ignorant "Red professors" were substituted for real scientists. In an elementary arithmetic textbook all the problems in addition, subtraction, multiplication, and division in which "a merchant sold so many apples for so many kopeks apiece" and the like were eliminated, as "counterrevolutionary and bourgeois." They were replaced by problems in which, for example, the Red Army was represented as killing so many counterrevolutionaries. Needless to say, this absurd "proletarianization" of science and mathematics was eventually abandoned, but the attempt itself is highly symptomatic of the prevailing spirit of the Communist rulers of that period.

With the beginning of the thirties a change began to take place in this attitude, imperceptible at first, and then rapidly gaining momentum. A keen appreciation of most cultural values came to replace the preceding negativistic position. In 1936, on the centenary of the death of Pushkin, the government organized hundreds of official festivals and thousands of public meetings in his honor, ordered the republication of his works, and extolled his genius in unprecedented terms. Communist books which had debunked him as "the mouthpiece of a degenerate aristocracy" were now declared to be anti-Communistic and counterrevolutionary. Authors, including Communists, who persisted in their earlier attitude were warned to cease their "counterrevolutionary nonsense." In short, a complete volte-face was effected.

The same generalization applies to other great Russian literature, as well as to celebrated musical dramas, and pictures, architectural structures (including churches valuable from the standpoint of the history of Russian architecture); and finally, to scientific, philosophical, religious, ethical, and juridical values. They all came to be highly appreciated and extolled. All attempts to debunk them were prohibited, their detractors being publicly reprimanded, denounced as counter-revolutionists, and sometimes punished.

The reaction to the first period of the Revolution went so far that most of the Marxian textbooks of Russian history were banned, especially those previously prescribed and written by the Commissar of Public Education, Pokrovski. These and similar works were replaced by texts that differed little from the elementary textbooks of Russian history used before the Revolution. Like the latter, they not only specifically mentioned but warmly praised illustrious Russian czars and princes, generals, economic organizers, inventors and scientists, artists, religious leaders, and so on, as creative geniuses and eminent builders of Russian civilization. Even a large number of books by Communist leaders, published in the first period, were now banned and withdrawn from circulation, being branded as "Trotskyist" or "wrong-line" publications.

Again, the motion pictures began to exalt certain personages who had been labeled "counterrevolutionists" during the first period. Such films as *Alexander Nevski* (shown in this country) and *Peter the Great* immortalized illustrious Russian princes and saints (like Alexander Nevski), czars (like Peter the Great and Alexander I), and czarist generals (like Suvorov and Kutuzov), as well as eminent — though highly conservative — Russian scientists (such as Lomonosov, Mendeleyeev, and Pavlov), notable economic organizers, etc.

In conformity with this volte-face, most of the social,

humanistic, and philosophical disciplines were reintroduced
into the university and high school curriculums; real scholars
were reinstated in their professional and research positions;
genuine experts began to replace the ignorant Communists in
economic activities, technology, science, education, the arts,
and even the military profession. A play entitled *The Front*,
by a Communist leader Alexander Korneytschuk, published
on August 25-27, 1942, in *Pravda* (the official organ of the
Communist party), is typical of the new cultural and practical
orientation. The villain of this play is the commander in chief
of "the Front," a prominent Communist named Gorloff, who
distinguished himself in the civil war. He is depicted as
thoroughly stupid and incompetent, self-seeking, and vain-
glorious. He is opposed by a group of young generals who have
played no role in the civil war, who occupy no official position
in the Communist party, and who can boast of no medals for
their revolutionary achievements. Gorloff is disgusted with
them for their disregard of his strategic plans and his military
orders. He threatens to punish them for their insubordination.
They calmly reply that his orders are incompetent; that his
achievements in the civil war are irrelevant to the exigencies
of this war; that he has grown "fat" resting on the laurels of his
revolutionary prowess; and that he must resign. Gorloff
naturally strips them of their rank and orders them to be
court-martialed. But at that moment an order comes from
Moscow dismissing Gorloff and appointing one of these
generals as commander in chief in his place.

Such a play, written by a Communist, published in *Pravda*,
and staged in Russia, is symbolic of the radical change undergone by the Revolution in regard to practically all the authentic values of Russian culture. The temporary submergence of
these values during the first stage of the Revolution is now
definitely at an end, the Communist attempts to replace the
historical culture of Russia by a spurious fiat culture having
proved futile,

The completion of this cycle means *a fundamental trans-formation of the Russian mentality and psychology, which diverges sharply from that of the first period of the Revolution and is developing in conformity to the vital trends of the pre-revolutionary era.* What was moribund in this field prior to the Revolution is dead; what was vigorous has revived and is flourishing. Gone is the psychology of class hatred fostered during the first period of the Revolution, having been replaced by a deep conviction of national unity and of the solidarity of all classes and groups. In the first period the very terms "patriotism," "Russia," "fatherland," "motherland" were sus-pect. The favorite watchwords were "Long live the Proletari-at!" "the Communist International," and similar slogans. These mottoes are now forgotten. The Communist Interna-tional is dissolved. Even in the official orders of Stalin, like that of May 1, 1943 (Order No. 195), we read: "Long live our glorious Motherland! Long live our valiant Red Army! Long live our valiant Navy! Long live our gallant men and women guerrillas! Death to the German invaders!" instead of "Long live Communism, the Proletariat, the Third International!" or "Death to capitalism and the bourgeoisie!" Appeals to national patriotism have replaced those of proletarian solidarity or international Communism. Appeals to national unity are sub-stituted for those of class disunity. This transformation was already under way several years before the outbreak of the war.

When this cycle of the Revolution is understood, a host of facts otherwise incomprehensible become intelligible and fall into their proper place, like the pieces of a complex jigsaw puzzle.

From the Communist Red Army to the Russian National Army. Many people have been surprised by the heroism and extraordinary fighting spirit of the Red Army, by the ability of its generals, by the comparative technical preparedness of Russia, at the unbounded sacrifices made by the Russian nation during the struggle and by a host of other unexpected military characteristics of Russia. We all know how egregiously its army was underrated by almost all the foreign specialists, as well as by Hitler and his generals. Confronted with its unexpected power, many are bewildered and cannot account for it. Others — a host of superficial reporters — explain it in terms of the magic of the Revolution. According to these "observers," up to the time of the Revolution Russia possessed no army, generals, or military equipment worth mentioning. All these, they contend, were produced by waving the magic wand of the Revolution. It is hardly necessary to point out the utter absurdity of such views. A little thought would have made it perfectly clear that the mere fact of the survival of Russia and its expansion into one of the greatest empires would have been impossible if from the beginning of its history it had lacked a strong, well-equipped army, directed by first-class military leaders, and if the nation had not been well organized for defense. Russia is an open plain, stretching across eastern Europe and Asia. This plain is devoid of natural barriers, such as oceans, seas, or impassable mountains. It has been incessantly invaded by Asiatic as well as European would-be conquerors. If, in spite of this fact, Russia has not been destroyed; if almost all the invasions have been repelled and the invaders defeated; if after some twelve centuries of its history Russia is still on the map — and very much so — this means that it has been able, on the whole, to organize its military defense successfully, possessing a first-class army, with first-class fighters, leaders, and equipment. Those who are familiar with the military history of Russia know that it has been as glorious as that of any other country; that victory has attended its military efforts as frequently as those of any other nation; that it has possessed as distinguished military leaders as those of any other army. The names of Sviatoslav, Dimitri Donskoi, Ivan the Terrible, Alexander Nevski, Peter the Great,

Suvorov, Kutuzov, and Skobelev rank with those of the foremost military leaders in European history.

To sum up. It is only to those who know nothing of the Russian Army and people as fighters and nothing of the military history of their country that the stubbornness, fortitude, heroism, and fighting genius of the Red Army are a surprise or enigma or the result of the magic of the Revolution. Those familiar with Russian military history are aware that these qualities are substantially in line with the centuries-long national military tradition of the country, though falling measurably short of it.[3]

The Red Army of the first period of the Revolution was very weak, incapable of resisting the armed forces of any strong nation or even the comparatively feeble armies of Poland and Finland or of the already partly disorganized Germany of 1918. The initial Red Army was defeated many times by numerically insignificant detachments of the so-called White Army. This weakness was precisely the reason why it began to be reorganized as early as 1921 or 1922 along the lines of the national army of Russia; why former Czarist generals were invited by the Communist Government to undertake this reorganization; why it was recruited, as before the Revolution, by means of universal conscription instead of through the voluntary induction of "proletarians." Since that time the task of rebuilding the national army has been relentlessly pursued by the Soviet Government and the Russian nation up to the

[3] After the Tatar invasion, in none of the major conflicts in which Russia was engaged was the enemy permitted to penetrate as deeply and to occupy as large and vital a portion of the country as the German Army has managed to do during the present war. Even the somewhat weakened Czarist Army of the first World War succeeded in halting the enemy near the borders of the empire. Only in the "Times of Trouble" at the beginning of the seventeenth century, when anarchy and revolution had seriously undermined Russia, were its foes able (chiefly by diplomatic rather than by purely military means) to penetrate approximately as deeply as did the Axis troops in this war. In both cases the disaster was due primarily to the crippling of the nation by protracted anarchy and revolution.

very outbreak of the present conflict. In this reconstruction (involving the hierarchy of ranks, the organization and discipline of the rank and file, and the various technical and other modifications demanded by contemporary war) the guiding influences have been the glorious traditions of the Russian Army, the heroic deeds of its past leaders, and love for the fatherland or motherland (*not* for "Communism" or "the Proletariat"). Until recently there remained one important Communist feature — namely, the use of political commissars who accompanied the army with a view to ensuring its loyalty to the Communist bosses. But even this feature was abolished soon after the crucial test of the war came. Today the so-called Red Army is actually the Russian national army. Its leaders and generals are the successors of the great Russian warriors of the past, following in their footsteps and emulating their deeds and their spirit.

The restoration of the national army of Russia is now about completed. Symbolically this is demonstrated by two recent innovations — unimportant in themselves, but highly suggestive for our purposes. About a year ago the Soviet Government introduced three new supreme military orders of decoration for heroism. These are known as the Order of Alexander Nevski, that of Suvorov, and that of Kutuzov. Up to that time the only similar orders had been the Order of Lenin, of a Hero of Socialist Labor, and certain others distinctively revolutionary in origin and name. Now, side by side with decorations inherently connected with the Revolution, we see the emblems of a celebrated prince, warrior, and saint of the thirteenth century (Alexander Nevski); of the Czarist general Suvorov, one of the foremost military geniuses of all times; and of another Czarist general, Kutuzov, the conqueror of Napoleon. What an incongruous combination — the order of Lenin side by side with the orders of a saint and prince and of Czarist generals! Such strange bedfellows are not uncommon in the second period of a revolution.

Still more significant is another feature, reintroduced in 1943 by the Soviet Government — the use of epaulets for military ranks. At the beginning of the Communist Revolution, epaulets were torn from any one who chanced to wear them, and the wearer was likely to be killed or at least arrested. They were viewed as a symbol of the odious Czarist and capitalist regimes — as a badge of counterrevolution. With the ascendance to power of the Communist rulers they were abolished from the army — seemingly forever. But in 1943 they reappeared, introduced by Stalin and the Soviet Government. The Soviet press enthusiastically praises the reform, and Soviet photographers are delighted to take pictures of generals of the Red Army displaying the novelty on their shoulders. Even Stalin himself began in 1943 to appear publicly in a resplendent uniform of Marshal of the Soviet Union instead of his hitherto simple semi-civilian costume.

These reforms are symbolic. They show clearly what has happened to the Communist Army of the first period of the Revolution. It has given place to the National Army of Russia, heroically fighting and dying not for Communism, not for the Third International, not even for the "world revolution" or the elimination of capitalism, but for the dear old motherland, Holy Russia, just as its predecessors used to fight and die for it. And the ci-devant Communist Stalin is now the chief of this national army. The cycle is virtually completed in this field.

From Communist Dictatorship to National Democracy and Then to War Dictatorship. What has been said of the army may be said, with the proper modifications, of almost all the main institutions of the present Soviet Union. The profound change which the *structure of the central government* has undergone since the first period of the Revolution is marked by the new Soviet Constitution of 1936. In all its essentials the structure of the government under this constitution is explicitly democratic, in contrast to that of the Communist dictatorship (alias "Proletarian Dictatorship" or "Third International"). To be sure, the new constitution has remained largely a theoretical reform; its provisions having been realized only in part, owing to the short period that has elapsed since its enactment. With the outbreak of the war, further application of its provisions necessarily ceased, just as the normal democratic regime ceased to function in all the belligerent countries. Its place was taken by a war regime which was bound to be rather dictatorial. However, the present regime is not a dictatorship of the proletariat or of the Communist party; it is a national dictatorship, engaged in waging a gigantic war. Observing its nature and its activities, one can discover hardly anything Communistic or proletarian except the names of its leaders and that of the Communist (or, as it is now officially called, Bolshevist) party. The names are old; but the policies which the leaders pursue and the activities which they direct are nationalist through and through.

The Revival of Prerevolutionary Foreign Policy. Since the middle of the thirties the *foreign policy* of Stalin has been merely a continuation of the foreign policy pursued by the Czarist regime during the periods of its vigor. Hence it is not surprising that, as in the Czarist days, Stalin's policy should have resulted in a series of explicit and implicit conflicts with the traditional enemy, Japan; that it led to good relations with China; that it decreed a preventive war with Finland as a protection against more powerful enemies; that it brought Russia into the same circle of allies with which she was associated during the First World War, in conflict with the same principal enemy, Germany; that, finally, Stalin and the Russian people want to recover such territories as Bessarabia, the Baltic provinces, and the preponderantly Russian portions of Poland, which, after having belonged to Russia for one or more centuries, were wrested from her during a period of weakness, being assigned partly to Rumania and partly to Poland or else set up as independent states (such as Latvia and Estonia). This partition of Russia after the First World War was not only a mistake but an act of gross perfidy toward a country which had saved its allies and had made greater sacrifices than any of its partners. If no new world order emerges after this war — if the international anarchy of a multitude of egoistic sovereign states continues — Russia will certainly have every right to reannex these lost possessions. Stalin's policy in these matters is unquestionably backed by the people, constituting a national policy par excellence.

Change in Economic Organization. The same decline of strictly Communistic trends in favor of national trends has been progressing, in the internal policy of the Soviet Government, not only in regard to the family, religion, the army, and culture in general but also in the field of *economic reorganization.* In the economic and financial fields several *strictly Communistic and equalitarian* innovations, introduced immediately after the outbreak of the Revolution, had to be abandoned as early as the years 1919-1922. First of all, there was the policy of *strict economic equality of income and plane of living,* which the Communist Government attempted to put into practice immediately after its accession to power. By 1918 it had admitted the ratio of 175 to 100 between the highest and the lowest wages of the laborers. In 1919 it had to go still further in the direction of inequality, enacting a decree fixing more than thirty different scales of wages and income. In 1921 the principle of equality was explicitly abandoned and replaced by that of "proportionality of remuneration to the efficiency of the work performed." Since that time inequality, in various forms, has grown until by 1940 certain groups, such as high officials, artists, scientists, and engineers, were enjoying incomes many hundreds of times larger than those of the mass of the population. Within the laboring class itself wages differed sharply according to personal efficiency and other factors. The so-called Stakhanovite principle of stimulating efficiency by a corresponding sliding scale of remuneration was fostered by every means. In a word, Communist equalitarianism soon died a natural death.

The second Communist novelty, attempted during the first years of the Revolution, was the *elimination of money and its replacement by a natural "ration system"*: to everyone according to his or her needs. Since the Soviet currency had depreciated to such an extent that it had lost almost all its value, such a radical reform was more than comprehensible. But it failed to work. Therefore, as early as 1922, the Soviet Government invited Kutler, a former Czarist minister of finance, and several other financial experts, to undertake the task of monetary reconstruction. This task was carried out, and since that time the Soviet monetary system has been functioning as well as could be expected. No further efforts to eliminate the use of money have been made.

As early as 1921 the Communistic economic system faced a grave crisis. Partly as a result of the First World War, and owing to the civil war and the Communist policy, Russia was brought to a state of hopeless misery and ruin. This condition, together with ever-mounting revolts of the population against the Soviet Government, forced the regime to abandon its Communist policies and to introduce what was officially styled the New Economic Policy (NEP). The NEP was an abrupt retreat from Communist economy toward a system intermediate between communism and capitalism.

Since that time the Soviet economic policy has undergone several transformations. Its main trend has been the rapid industrialization of the country carried through by the central government with a planned utilization of the most advanced technological methods. This trend was complicated by the paramount considerations of military preparedness, which entailed enormous expenditures for armaments and heavy industries. These objectives forced the government to collectivize the peasants; to cut to a bare minimum (bordering on poverty or actual starvation) the standard of living of the population; to make its five-year plans of economic reconstruction; and to introduce a host of other painful measures. If no revolution had occurred, industrialization would have been effected — probably even more successfully — without all these violent measures. Under the conditions of the Revolution the rudest coercion, involving the acute suffering of untold millions, was inevitable for the accomplishment of this task.

By 1940, as we have seen, Russia had come to occupy virtually second place among the industrial nations of the world. A system of heavy industry had been created. There appeared now a possibility of undertaking the production of consumers' goods on a large scale, and thus of very substantially raising, within a short time, the standard of living of the masses. If there had been no war, within a decade or so the standard of living would undoubtedly have risen very notably. Unfortunately, the war not only halted this process but turned almost all of European Russia and a part of Asiatic Russia into something resembling a cemetery. Cities and villages, fields and factories, were laid waste, encumbered with corpses and with the charred remnants of what had been prosperous agricultural and industrial communities. For the second time in this century war had prevented Russia from achieving a high economic plane of living. Such in outline has been the recent transformation of Russia's economic organization.

This "étatisme" (from the French "état," "state,") or governmentally controlled and managed economy, in itself is neither communistic nor capitalistic. It has been practiced many times before, in the most conservative countries of the remote past, such as ancient Egypt under the Pharaohs — a regime as far removed from Communism as possible. It was the basic economic system of Ptolemaic Egypt; of ancient Sparta; of Lipara; of ancient Rome after the third century A.D.; of Byzantium throughout almost its entire history; as well as of the Inca state of Peru. It was practiced during certain epochs in China, and in various other countries, under regimes having no relationship to Communism. As I have shown elsewhere,[4] such a system of *étatisme* regularly emerges during acute social emergencies such as war, revolution, famine, and pestilence, flourishes as long as the emergency conditions prevail, and tends to decline when the emergency passes. This sociological law is one of the most solid and valid generalizations of the social sciences. In its light it is quite comprehensible why such an overdeveloped *étatisme* arose in Russia; and why since the outbreak of the present conflict all the belligerent countries (including the United States, Great Britain, and the other democracies) have greatly expanded state control, management, and regulation of all the economic affairs of the nation, drastically curtailing the functions of private persons and groups in this field. We do not call our governmentally controlled and managed economy Communistic; nor is the Soviet system of economy essentially Communistic in character. It is simply *étatisme*.

As a matter of fact, *there is now scarcely any fundamental difference between the Soviet and American systems of wartime economy.* Their similarities are far greater than their dissimilarities. The main objection to this statement is that whereas in the United States we recognize the existence of private property, the Soviet system does not recognize it. Formally the objection is to a certain extent valid. On closer examination, however, the difference in the status of property in the two countries appears less conspicuous than the statement implies. First of all, personal economic values, or consumers' goods, are owned, used, and disposed of in much the same way in Russia as in America. The principal difference between the two systems relates almost exclusively to the means and instruments of large-scale production.

As regards this kind of economic values there is no private property in Russia. They belong to the nation. But today

[4] Cf. my *Man and Society in Calamity*, chap. vii; *Social and Cultural Dynamics*, Vol. III, chap. vii; and *Sociology of Revolution*, Parts III and IV.

there is little private property of this type even in the United States, where the overwhelming majority of the large-scale means of production are in the hands of the corporations, like the United States Steel Corporation, General Motors, the General Electric, and so on. In 1930 the two hundred largest corporations controlled approximately 38 per cent of the business wealth and 22 per cent of the total wealth of the country. The totality of existing corporations possessed the greater part of its wealth and almost all the economic means of production.

The status of the property held by the corporations is very different from that of private property in the classic sense of the term. The latter implies the right of the owner to possess, use, manage, and dispose of the value in question. In the case of a corporation these various functions are split: those who theoretically own its property — the thousands of shareholders — neither possess it, nor use it, nor manage it, nor dispose of it. Conversely, those who manage and often dispose of it — the board of directors or managers — do not own it: in the two hundred biggest corporations none of the presidents or directors owned even 1 per cent of its shares in 1930. Then full-fledged private property in the classic sense of the term, especially in the field of large-scale production, was given the first fatal blow by the corporations, which have been rapidly expanding, hence absorbing an ever-increasing part of the wealth of the country. When, finally, supreme control of corporation as well as private property was assumed, during the war, by the government of the United States, the next step was taken in the elimination of full-fledged private property, and a system of *étatisme* was adopted similar to that prevailing in the Soviet Union.

The status of property so far as instruments of production are concerned is not very different in the Soviet Union from the structure of corporation economy in the United States as outlined above. All the means of production on a large scale belong to the Russian nation. Their supreme control and management are vested in the Soviet Government. But just as in this country they are divided among various corporations, so in Russia they are allotted to many separate industrial branches or corporations. Each branch — say the steel industry — is managed by its board of directors; each individual factory, by its separate executives. The board of directors is endowed with a wide margin of independence and autonomy. The capital expenses and income, liabilities and assets, profits and deficit, of a given industry are a unit, virtually as independent of those of other industries, corporations, or factories as the capital and budget of the United States Steel Corporation are independent of those of the Radio Corporation of America. The board of managers of a Soviet industry or factory directs but does not own the property; similarly, in an American corporation the managers direct but do not own the corporation property. In neither country do the real owners — the Russian people and the hundreds of thousands of shareholders in the United States — manage what they theoretically own. Finally, the government exercises supreme control over all the corporate and noncorporate property.

Furthermore, in both countries a portion of the instruments of production (those on a small scale) are practically under the complete control of private persons and groups — for instance, such instruments as a horse or cow, a wagon or automobile, a small house or apartment, a kitchen garden, a plot of land, the tools of artisans and craftsmen, or the implements of artists, scientists, and professional workers. They are possessed, used, managed, and disposed of in much the same manner in Russia as in America. The main difference lies in the respective peasant and farmer ownership. In America — apart from tenants, share croppers, and laborers — the farms (if unmortgaged), together with their various appurtenances, belong to the individual cultivators. In Russia, since the collectivization of agriculture the right of ownership of land has been vested in the nation. But actually the land cultivated by this or that collective farm remains at its disposal, according to legal guarantees, forever (art. 8, of the *Standard Rules of an Artel*, decreed February 17, 1935). Each collective manages its own affairs autonomously, as an independent unit. Each member possesses his own "private property" — a plot of land for his personal use; horses or cows (from 1 to 10 cows, 10 to 150 sheep) or other domestic animals; and a dwelling house, side by side with the strictly communal buildings (such as a club, library, or school, offices, etc.). Likewise, for his work in the community he is remunerated in proportion to its amount and efficiency with many forms of bonuses. (Equality of remuneration was abandoned a number of years ago.)

With the exception of periods of emergency, when an agricultural worker may be temporarily "frozen" on a given farm or an industrial worker in a given factory (as is now being done in the United States during the war emergency), a member is free to leave the farm or the factory if he wishes to do so. On the other hand, one cannot be evicted from a collective farm except in case of crime or of flagrant violation of the farm rules, and, at least, two thirds of all members have to vote for such an eviction. The management of the collective farms was at first autocratic, the managers being appointed by the government. It is now democratic, the officers being elected by the collective farm community for a specific term. The plans for economic and cultural activities are discussed and determined by the totality of members in the supreme organ of the community at its general meeting. The land cannot be taken from the community or sold to anyone. It cannot become an object of profiteering or speculation or pass into the hands of commercial dealers and capitalists. All in all, *the present collective farm is merely a modernized form of an old national institution — the peasant "mir" and "obschina"* (discussed above), or a *variety of workers' productive co-operative society known to all countries and greatly developed in prerevolutionary Russia.* As we pass from 1930 to 1940 we observe that the personal rights of the members of the collective farms, their private property, their autonomy, even their inequality in respect to remuneration, have been steadily increasing, while the strictly Communistic traits imposed during the twenties have been progressively disappearing. As compared with the status of an American tenant, share-cropper, agricultural laborer, or even a farm owner with his farm mortgaged and in danger of foreclosure, the property rights of the Russian peasants are greater than those of the corresponding strata of the American agricultural population. In any case, the above outline shows that the collective farm has little to do with Communism and is essentially a modernized restoration of old peasant institutions — the *mir* and *obschina*. It combines well the advantages of large-scale production with intensive small farming. Freed from several defects it undoubtedly points out the best possible way to solve the land problem in many countries.

Thus, when we examine more closely the forms of ownership in Soviet Russia and in the United States we observe that they have tended to converge more and more and that they now differ much less than the formal statement of the recognition of private property here and its abolition in Russia implies. Full-fledged private property, in the sense of the right of the owner to possess, use, manage, and dispose of it, is greatly curtailed in both countries. It now exists mainly in the field of consumers' goods, personal income, and small-scale producers' goods. The bulk of the means of production are managed by those who do not own them; and their theoretical owners do not manage them. Thus the corporate property and economy of America is a twin brother of the corresponding corporations and units of nationalized industry in Russia. Here the corporations pay taxes to the nation and sell their produce to the consumers. In Russia they pay their taxes and sell their produce to the people. Here the corporation managers receive high salaries, partly at the expense of the shareholders. In Russia they receive possibly lower salaries and bonuses, at less cost to the nation. Here the marked success of a corporation may result in an increase in the wages, salaries, and bonuses paid to the employees. So also in Russia. In these and many other respects the supposedly capitalist economy of the American corporation is in fact a twin brother of the supposedly Communist economy of the industrial and agricultural units of Soviet Russia. Finally, in both countries the *government* is in business, and largely controls and manages the economic life of the nation. In Russia, between the first years of the Communist Revolution and 1940, governmental management and control of economic activities has tended to decrease. At the beginning of the Revolution this control was almost complete. Since then the amount of decentralization; the degree of private initiative, responsibility, and autonomy; the amount of private ownership of property; and the inequality of remuneration have steadily increased in all the state-owned and other enterprises. In the United States the trend has been the reverse, especially since the crash of 1929. The amount of governmental control and regimentation has systematically expanded, especially since our involvement in the war. Individual private property (in the classic sense) and full-blooded capitalism have rapidly declined; and there is no chance of restoring them to their nineteenth-century status, especially that of the precorporation economy. Thus in this field we note a progressive mutual convergence of the economic forms of the two countries. Hence the absurdity of the references to the unbridgeable gulf between the Russian "Communist" system and the American "Capitalist" system.

To sum up. In the economic field we observe the decline of the Communist system of the first period of the Revolution, and the resumption, in a modified form, of the trends that existed before the Revolution. These trends have been reenforced or modified, on the one hand by conditions of grave emergency, and, on the other, by the modern technology of production and economic management. Regardless of the personal predilections of the Communists and capitalists, and the bloody memories of the first phase of the Communist revolution, there is no impassable gulf or irreconcilable conflict between the present economy of Soviet Russia and that of the United States. Each has evolved a similar system of so-called "planned economy," with supreme control vested in the government, and with a managerial corporation bureaucracy that is progressively driving out the old-fashioned capitalist owners. A like change has taken place in virtually all the other highly industrialized countries, including the democracies.

The "Purge" of Communist Leaders by Communist Leaders. Finally, the *cycle of the Russian Revolution is clearly demonstrated by the purges of Communist leaders by Stalin and by the so-called Communist party.* Most of the leaders of the first period of the Revolution — including those who stood next to Lenin in the Communist hierarchy and became his successors, such as Trotski, Kamenev, Rykov, and Zinoviev, as well as hundreds of other eminent Communists like Bukharin (the "Thomas Aquinas of Communism"), Piatakov, and Karakhan — were "purged." Thousands were imprisoned or banished. Tens of thousands of lesser Communists were "excommunicated" from the unholy Church of Russian Communism. By whom? Not by counterrevolutionists or anti-Communists; not by Czarist generals or Western capitalists. No. They were executed, imprisoned, banished, or excommunicated by Stalin and the Communist party itself. To these should be awarded the first prize for the mortal blow dealt the Communist phase of the Revolution and Russian Communism in general.

Here we have one of the regular uniformities exhibited by practically all major revolutions. As an ancient observer put it,

"Revolution is a crocodile that devours first the rich and fat people; next the middle classes; then the poor and emaciated; and finally the revolutionaries themselves." This purge marks the drastic shift in the course of the Russian Revolution from its Communist to its non-Communist or even anti-Communist phase. The purely personal motives and causes, the intrigues and counterintrigues among the Communist leaders, were mere surface phenomena — mere personal reflections of the impersonal destiny of a profound revolution to pass from its "thesis" to its "antithesis" (to speak in Hegelian and Marxian terms). Most of the purged Communists did not heed this inexorable historical dictum: they tried to oppose the inevitable trend of the Revolution toward its nonrevolutionary and non-Communist phase. Trotski and others stubbornly sought to perpetuate the "permanent Communist Revolution" and to disseminate it over the entire world. They attempted to thwart its immanent destiny of self-liquidation and to prevent the inevitable revival of vital national trends — to oppose the imponderable but irresistible forces which have operated throughout the entire history of the Russian nation. As a result of this foolish (or, if you like, romantic and heroic) enterprise, they were ruthlessly brushed aside. *Volentem fata ducunt, nolentem trahunt.* Stalin and his followers, who had enjoyed much less prestige and power at the beginning of the Revolution — even in 1922 — than Trotski, Rykov, Kamenev, and Zinoviev, very easily disposed of them — not because they were more powerful, more capable or brilliant, than their opponents, but because, like Oliver Cromwell, the "Thermidorians," and other notable revolutionary leaders, Stalin and his followers (whether deliberately or otherwise) moved *with the current* of historical destiny and *not against it.* Hence their victory. Hence the objective character of their anti-Communist policy. Hence their paramount role in the cycle of the Russian Revolution. More than any other person or group of persons, Stalin and his associates contributed to the liquidation of the Communist phase of the Revolution (probably against their personal inclinations), and to the revival of the national trends of Russia. In this sense they have been lucky, if not actually wise and farseeing. If, like the purged Communist leaders, they had sought to stem the tide of historical destiny, they would have been brushed aside as easily as their victims. If in the future they should try to revive Communism as it existed in the first stage of the Revolution, they would be "liquidated" as inexorably as Trotsky and his adherents. That is why I do not worry about what Stalin or any other leader may think or do. If they continue to steer the ship of state with the current, they will perform a useful service, as they have done during the post-destructive stage of the Revolution, particularly in the prosecution of the war with Germany. If not, they will share the fate of other executives who have failed to heed the lessons of history. Finally the discussed trend is demonstrated also by a *restoration of law* and the *government by law* that were abolished in the first phase of the Revolution. (See about that M. Laserson. "Rehabilitation of Law in Soviet Russia." Novoie Rus. Slovo, Nov. 6, 1943.)

This chapter shows the fallacy of the supposedly convincing argument that there is an irreconcilable conflict between the Soviet and the American way of life. Actually, economically and politically, the two nations have been steadily converging toward a similar type of social organization and economy. Communism and the destructive period of the Revolution are already "corpses." Only political scavengers can be interested in their revival. Thoughtful, farseeing, creative persons and groups may, to be sure, feel a deep sense of compassion for the past tragedy of a great nation. But they do not seek to resuscitate a national "corpse." Rather, they take the existing reality and endeavor, to the best of their ability, to eliminate its defects and to realize its potential virtues. The new type of society emerging in this country as well as in Russia has many shortcomings, but it has also many potentialities for good. The development of its true values is the task of the living. In this constructive work the two nations can and will co-operate to their mutual advantage.

5. General Conclusion

This closes my thesis. I have shown that owing to the operation of certain impersonal factors, the two nations (apart from the destructive stage of the Russian Revolution) have had a unique record of long, unbroken peace and co-operation. I have indicated the nature of these factors — namely, the virtual absence of any irreconcilable conflict between the fundamental values of the two countries, and the positive fact of their essential sociocultural similarity or congeniality. I have pointed out these factors continue to operate. This presages still closer co-operation in the future — a welcome destiny, beneficial to both peoples and to the rest of mankind. It is refreshing to sense, within the otherwise dark and chaotic maze of events, so beneficent a destiny.

There remains only to try to delineate the two possible types of postwar reconstruction available to Russia and America and to the nations of the world. Let us now glance briefly at these problems.

6. The Roles of American-Russian Co-operation in the Post-war World

Assuming the continuation of friendly co-operation between the two nations in the future, its forms and functions will depend upon the nature of the postwar world. If it consists of a multitude of sovereign states, selfish and cynical, con-

travening the norms of decent moral conduct and exalting
raisons d'état as the paramount values, then the American-
Russian alliance will play essentially the same role as it has
played hitherto. But this state of affairs is recognized as
intolerable and if an earnest effort is made to abolish it — at
least to the extent of assuring a durable peace, and respect
for the elementary dignity of the individual — then this co-
operation will assume much more important and creative
functions.

Under the first assumption, it will produce a series of mutual
benefits, economic, military, and cultural. Without even diplomatic pressure the United States will strongly influence the
Soviet regime in the direction of terminating its dictatorial
violation of the elementary rights of Russian citizens — in
strengthening the "four freedoms" in Russia. On the other
hand, Russia will continue to fructify the culture — particularly the fine arts — of the United States; and it may facilitate
a decrease of the commercial hypocrisy, selfishness, and exploitation inherent, to a certain extent, in any private business
on a large scale.

Internationally their co-operation will contribute to the
preservation of peace; the mitigation of national and racial
inequalities; the termination of colonial exploitation; and the
bridging of the gulf between the West and the East, between
the so-called "civilized" and "uncivilized" peoples. It will also
promote the development of essential industries in many backward regions by the people of such regions, and in their
interest in contradistinction to that of foreign capitalists.
Finally, both nations can do a great deal in diffusing a spirit
of universal brotherhood. In case of the outbreak of international war, the alliance of these countries will greatly
strengthen each partner in coping with the emergency.

If, however, the millions of victims of the present war are
not to have died in vain — if an earnest attempt is made to
create a nobler and better world, and if this new order aims to

secure for mankind a lasting peace and a decent minimum of economic and cultural benefits — then the co-operation of the two nations may play a decisive role. If they consecrate themselves wholeheartedly and unreservedly to this exalted purpose, if they combine the highest idealism with the most practical realism (the innocence of a dove with the wisdom of a serpent), if they embark upon this magnificent adventure with a full realization not only of its long-time advantages but also of the temporary sacrifices which it entails, then their leadership may mark the advent of the greatest era in the entire history of mankind. Given the unflinching determination of the two nations to initiate the construction of this new world, the rest of mankind will gladly follow their leadership. If one or few recalcitrant nations should try to oppose it, their puny and shameful efforts will be easily brushed aside.

The disintegration of the whole fabric of contemporary culture has reached a critical stage. The suicidal forces of destruction have attained the proportions of a devastating tornado. The list of victims of the international and civil wars of this century is unprecedented in the annals of the human race. A continuation of the "old order" is hence out of the question. The creation of a new order is on the agenda of history. It is demanded in the interest of the preservation not only of civilization and culture but of humanity itself. We face an ultimatum: Either persist in the effort to retain the old order and thereby perish or, in spite of its superhuman difficulties, undertake to build a new order. The peoples — and especially the governments and rulers — of the world have to choose one of these alternatives. It is to be hoped that Russia and America will make the right choice. The realization of a durable international and national peace and of truly humane conditions for all mankind is the most urgent task of our time. In order that this task may be achieved, the *causes* of war and oppression must be eliminated. The fundamental causes of the disintegration of contemporary culture and of the exploitation of human beings have been discussed elsewhere.[5] The basic causes and factors of war and of lasting peace are discussed in the next two chapters.

[5] Cf. my *Social and Cultural Dynamics, The Crisis of Our Age,* and *Man and Society in Calamity.*

CHAPTER TEN

THE CAUSE AND FACTORS OF WAR AND PEACE

1. *Main Cause Versus Multiple Causation*

In order that a diagnosis of the preconditions of peace may be precise and fruitful, we must distinguish between the *main or necessary cause of peace and its supplementary factors, both positive and negative.* By the main or necessary condition is meant the factor without which peace cannot prevail. By the supplementary factors are meant the numerous and diverse conditions that either facilitate the realization of the effects of the necessary cause or neutralize them. Thus, in diphtheria the necessary cause is infection. Positive supplementary factors are those conditions favoring the spread of germs and decreasing the immunity of the human organism to infection; negative supplementary factors are inoculation and similar influences that neutralize or inhibit the *effects* of infection, thereby turning the necessary cause into an *insufficient* cause. The necessary cause of birth is conception. The positive supplementary factors are all the conditions that favor the growth of the foetus into a child. Negative supplementary conditions are those which, like abortion, and disease, inhibit this development of the foetus. The main cause of a given phenomenon is always the same, but the supplementary factors are diverse, variable, and shifting in their nature as well as in their combinations.

I am perfectly aware of the many objections against distinguishing between the necessary cause and the supplementary factors. These objections can be found in almost all the serious treatises on inductive logic, such as those by J. S. Mill, A. A. Tshuprov, J. Venn, C. Sigwart, and others, as well as in a number of special monographs on causality. However, the logical and investigational advantages of such a distinction are so great, and its disadvantages are so comparatively small, that the objections can be disregarded. They are really far from decisive. The principle of the main cause and supplementary factors is generally used in causal analysis throughout the natural sciences. Their experience confirms its validity and fruitfulness. Nearly all the advances in the natural sciences have involved the discovery of the main or necessary cause of a given phenomenon, and some of its supplementary factors.

Without such a procedure we are hopelessly lost in almost any causal analysis of sociocultural phenomena in general, and of war and peace in particular. The "multiple-factor" theory of war (or peace) looks nice on paper, especially when it is given a mathematical appearance: "War is a function of the variables A, B, C, ... M [$W=f(A, B, C, ... M)$]." But as soon as the formula is applied to real variables it becomes either meaningless nonsense or a denial of causation. It results in an infinite regression leading either to a "Prime Mover" or to the proposition that the whole world is the cause of everything. First, it is impossible to describe the countless antecedent conditions of a particular war or of war in general. Secondly, if such a description were possible, it would not clarify the causes of war at all, because it would remain but an incomplete catalogue of millions of conditions without any distinction as to which of these are causal and which are incidental. Third, if the theory of multiple causation means a selection of a few of the myriad circumstances amidst which war occurs, the choice is bound to be perfectly arbitrary. The selected variables would be so heterogeneous, incommensurable, and noncomparable that no one could combine them into a meaningful unity. Still less could one measure their relative causative power.

Suppose, from the countless antecedent conditions of World War I we select the vicissitudes of the Czarist regime in Russia, the shot at Sarajevo, the visit of Poincaré to Russia in the summer of 1914, heterogeneous composition of the Hapsburg empire, the peculiarities of the psychology of Viscount Gray or of Wilhelm Hohenzollern, the rainy season in some part of central Europe, Germany's expansionist policy, the state of the sunspots, and the Franco-English-Russian alliance. Anyone who puts these or other heterogeneous variables into one formula produces nothing but a meaningless collection of words or symbols without any sense or unity. We cannot measure the relative causal role of any of these incommensurable factors. Hence, the theory of multiple causation is not applicable to sociocultural phenomena generally, or to the study of war and peace in particular.[1] It is far more inadequate than the theory of a main cause and supplementary factors. This explains why I use the latter in preference to the former.

2. *The Main Cause of Internal and International Peace*

1. *The main cause of internal social peace is the presence in the given society of a well-integrated system of basic values, with their corresponding norms of conduct.[2] The fundamental values of the various factions and members of the society must be essentially in harmony with this system and with one another.*

2. *The main cause of international peace is the presence in each of the interacting societies of a well-integrated system of ultimate values and their norms, all of which are compatible with one another.*

[1] See a development of this criticism of multiple causation and of other pseudo-mathematical procedures in my *Sociocultural Causality, Space, Time* (Duke University Press, 1943).

[2] Every basic value has its set of norms of conduct; with their "thou shall" and "thou shall not." Religious, ethico-juridical, scientific, economic, political, aesthetic values — each has its code of conduct.

3. In a given universe of societies or within a particular society the probability of peace varies directly with the integration of the systems of the basic values and their mutual compatibility. When their integration and harmoniousness decline, especially suddenly and sharply, the chances for international or civil war increase.

Before elaborating these propositions, a few clarifying comments are in order.

A. Our attention is focused on the main values and not on the minor values of the given societies. What exactly are the major values of any society must be found by factual investigation. In general, they are composed of the basic ethico-juridical, religious, scientific, economic, political, and aesthetic values and those of self-respect and independence. This does not prevent different societies from stressing now religious, now economic, now political values as *primus inter pares.* In spite of such concrete differences from society to society and from period to period, these values are generally fundamental ones.

B. We speak not of this or that specific value, but of a system of all the primary values. Where the main values are integrated, they make one unified system in which they are all meaningfully interconnected and causally interdependent. When one of the basic values of a society becomes incompatible with certain main values of another society, the whole system of one becomes irreconcilable with the system of the other. In the causation of either peace or war, this or that isolated value does not operate alone, but the system of major values as a whole is the effective unit.

C. By integration of the main values is meant their meaningful-causal interdependence — meaningful in the sense that they are logically or aesthetically consistent, articulating the same values, principles, and norms in different ways; causal in the sense that when one of them changes notably, the rest also change. When the whole system experiences a transmutation each of the main values undergoes a corresponding transformation. Values that do not have this meaningful-causal interdependence remain unintegrated; those losing their previous integration become disintegrated.[3]

D. Finally, we are concerned with the compatibility of the systems of values but not with their similarity, homogeneity or identity. The point is that two systems of values may be heterogeneous and yet not incompatible with one another. In a society like ours, the citizens have different religions, aesthetic tastes, and political ideas. Yet they are compatible with one another, and their heterogeneity does not lead to civil war.

Having clarified these propositions, we may ask what are the evidences of their validity.

3. Evidence of the Validity of the Propositions

The following negative and positive corroborations can be mentioned. Each of these sets of evidence sums up a fairly regularly repeated uniformity, and therefore is a more adequate proof than a mere collection of singularistic facts. Let us begin with the series of negative corroborations.[4]

Negative Evidences. By negative proofs are meant those uniformities that exhibit either an *explosion or increase of war whenever the integration of the main values and their compatibility decrease. If this decrease occurs among the factions and members of a given society, the result is civil war or severe and bloody punishment. If the decrease of integration and harmony occurs among the value-systems of different societies the result is international war.*

[3] See on this my *Dynamics*, Vol. IV, chaps. i, ii, iii.
[4] Factual data for corroboration can be found in my *Social and Cultural Dynamics* (New York, 1937-41), Vol. III, chaps. ix-xiv; and in Quincy Wright, *A Study of War* (Chicago University Press, 1942), Vol. I, II.

A. The first set of negative corroborations consists of the *countless outbreaks of war when two hitherto isolated societies, with different systems of values, come for the first time into direct and durable contact.* The contact makes real the potential irreconcilability of their contrasting main values. According to the proposition, such a situation must lead to war, and it has done so fairly uniformly, in ancient as well as in more recent times. Quincy Wright's study shows that the warfare of comparatively isolated peoples has the lowest mean index (2.03); next come peoples with moderate inter-cultural contacts (index 2.59); finally the peoples with wide and close cultural contacts (index 2.91).[5] Early history and anthropology gives us hundreds of cases of wars occasioned by the meeting of two formerly isolated tribes. If their basic values were different such a contact has almost invariably been followed by warfare. The same is true of historical socie-ties. A notable portion of the wars of these societies occurred precisely when, in the process of migration or expansion or colonization, one society met another for the first time. The contact was almost invariably followed by wars whether of defence, offense, misunderstanding, subjugation, or coloniza-tion, even when the societies had no conscious military objec-tives. So it was in history of Egypt, Babylonia, China and Persia, Greece and Rome, Europe and America. When Egyp-tians met Nubians or Palestinians or Hyksos or any other group with different values, war followed. When in the process of peaceful colonization the Greeks met other peoples and societies war took place. The same is true of the Macedon-ians and the Romans throughout their history. The expan-sion of these empires meant contact with other societies hav-ing different systems of values. The resultant wars lasted until one part was destroyed or subjugated, or their values became compatible. The same is true when West met East; when the Spaniards met the aboriginal Americans, and so on

[5] Quincy Wright, *op. cit.*, p. 559. See also table 12, on p. 557.

through the chronic colonial wars that have been going on continually.

B. This partly explains why the *rapid expansion of contact and communication after the thirteenth century has been followed by an increase of war on this planet. New technical means of communication and transportation* have brought face to face an ever increasing number of tribes, societies, nations, and empires. The irreconcilability of their value-systems was thus systematically intensified. Consequently wars, especially colonial conflicts, increased until, in the nineteenth century, the truly isolated groups had almost disappeared. They all were subjugated by force and then divided between the great powers.

In all these wars the real cause is not the fact of contact and expansion of intersocietal interaction. By themselves contact and interaction as such are not the cause of diphtheria: a person can have thousands of contacts with other persons and still be free from diphtheria. He may be in touch with a sick person and yet remain healthy as long as he does not get the infection. The cause is infection by the germs; contact is a facilitating circumstance. Similarly, intersocietal contact and interaction do not lead to war, if the value systems of the respective societies are not incompatible. The cause is the incompatibility. Social contact and interaction are facilitating factors.

C. *The third set of corroborations is given by civil wars arising from a rapid and fundamental change in the ultimate values of one part of a given society while the other part either does not undergo it or moves in the opposite direction.* This means a rapid increase in the incompatibility of the main values of the two parts of the society. According to the present thesis, some sort of civil strife should follow such a transformation. And this has uniformly been the case. Practically all the civil wars of the past have emerged from a sudden increase of the contrast in the major values of revolutionaries and counterrevolutionaries. From the civil wars of Egypt and Persia to the recent upheavals of Russia and Spain, history consistently offers evidence of the validity of our proposition.

D. *The fourth set of proofs consists of the cases where in the universe of interacting societies a profound transformation of the value-systems occurs only in one or a few without occurring simultaneously in the other interacting societies.* Such a situation means again a greater incompatibility of the values of these societies. The result of such an increase has uniformly been an outbreak of war between the societies involved. Take, for instance, the historical cases of profound religious transformation. When Achenaton's religious revolution occurred in ancient Egypt, the result was civil and then international war. When the Buddhist religious transformation occurred in India, a similar series of conflicts followed. The emergence of Christianity, the Byzantian iconoclastic reformation, and the Protestant Reformation each resulted in a long series of wars. The same is true of such religious variations of Christianity as the Hussite movement and the Albigensian "heresy." The story has been repeated many times in human history with monotonous uniformity.

If the transformation occurs in the realm of *political* or *politico-economic* values, it assumes the form of a political or politico-economic revolution. If the changes in one society are sufficiently radical, they are generally followed by a series of "revolutionary wars" with the unrevolutionized neighbors. The wars of the Cromwellian, French, Russian, and Nazi revolutions are typical illustrations of the uniformity. There are few profound political or economico-political revolutions in history without their aftermath of war.

E. A fifth group of proofs is epitomized by the *fact of the increase of war attendant upon an acceleration of sociocultural change in a given universe of interacting societies. This is especially true in the West and throughout the world during the last five centuries.* The real cause of an increase of war in such periods is not *acceleration*. If it proceeds at an orderly and uniform pace in all societies, no intensified irreconcilability of the value-systems occurs, and therefore no internal or external war follows. This is witnessed, for instance, by the rapid rate of change in Europe and America during the second part of the nineteenth century. Variation in the tempo of change *per se* is neither a war-making nor a peace-making factor. It is neutral. If it promoted war in certain cases, the reason is that not all the societies changed at the same rate. This made for greater incompatibility in their value-systems; hence the increase of bloody conflicts. During rapid change the main values are in a state of flux and do not have time to "settle" and become universal; they become somewhat disintegrated, thereby further facilitating war.

F. The sixth category of evidence includes the following facts. Empires composed of highly heterogeneous and conflicting populations and cultures often initiate wars in order to prevent a development of internal movements threatening their unity. In cases of this kind the incompatibility first manifests itself internally, in the form of struggle and civil war. This eventually provokes international war.

G. We next consider the opposite instance, where the nation is perfectly integrated internally. In other words, it is highly nationalistic. But being thus unified, it differs fundamentally from other societies with respect to its system of values. Its norms are incompatible with theirs. An ultra-nationalistic state does not respect or tolerate its neighbors' ways. The uniform result of such arrogance and intolerance has been war.

In both of these cases the cause of the wars is not heterogeneity or homogeneity *per se*. In different situations they could lead to other results. In the situations described they lead to war because they produce a clash of the values of the given societies.

H. The eighth series of corroborations involves the *major*

movements in the magnitude of war in the history of Greece, Rome, and European countries, as it is given in my pioneer study and now in the quoted work of Quincy Wright. Both studies agree in practically all essential points and so far there is no other systematic investigation of the problem. The major fluctuations of these curves cannot be accounted for by any hypothesis except the one proposed herein. (See diagram No. 1) *According to our hypothesis we should expect the greatest magnitude of war, measured by the casualties per million of the population, in the periods of radical transformation of the main values of the societies.* That is exactly what these curves show.

In Greece the most belligerent centuries are the fourth and fifth B.C.[6] We know that these centuries saw a most profound and rapid transformation of the value-system of Greek society. The old religious or ideational system was crumbling, the new sensate system was not yet built. All Greece was in a state of immense flux.[7] No value or norm remained universally binding for all states, groups, or individuals. Complete sociocultural *anomie* became supreme. In these conditions the incompatibility of the common values enormously increased.

When values cease to be universally binding, their controlling power evaporates. Human beings and groups become dominated mainly by blind, egotistic, biological impulses. Brute force supplemented by fraud becomes supreme. It would be a miracle if under these circumstances wars and civil strife did not enormously increase. Indeed, war reached its highest level in Greek history during these centuries.

The most belligerent centuries in the history of Rome were the third and first B.C. and the third A.D.[8] Why? The third century witnessed the long and bloody conflict between irreconcilable value-systems of Rome and Carthage. The first cen-

---

[6] See the detailed data in my *Dynamics*, Vol. III.
[7] For the facts and details see the four volumes of my *Dynamics*
[8] See the data and indices in *Dynamics*, Vol. III.

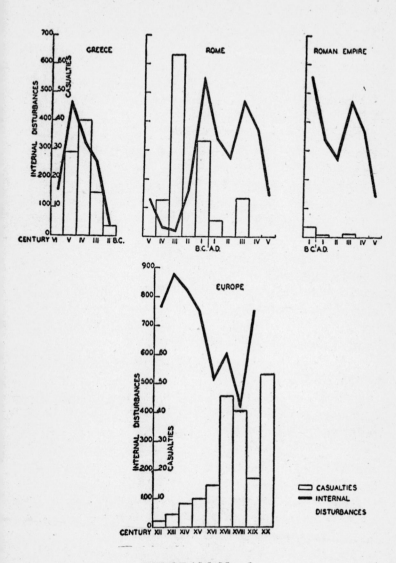

DIAGRAM No. 1

tury B.C. saw the great transmutation of the formerly semi-ideational values of Rome to an overripe sensate form. The transformation was enormously accelerated by the impact of the sensate Hellenic culture upon the Roman society. At the end of the second and during the first century B.C. as in Greece, it led to *anomie*. In this situation as we would expect, an increase of civil and international wars occurred. Finally, a rise of the "curve" in the third century A.D. is again quite comprehensible. In the third century A.D. Christianity, with its ideational system of values sharply opposed to the dominant sensate system, came to the surface as a tangible power. The struggle between the pagan (sensate) and Christian (ideational) systems assumed public form. Hence, according to the proposition, war had to increase. (For the next few centuries no reliable data are available.)

If we take eight main European countries and study the most belligerent periods of their history, the results are similar. Their war maxima fall in the periods of increasing incompatibility and disintegration of the value-systems.[9] Without going into details for each country, we can summarize the movement of war in Europe as whole, from the twelfth century to 1925.

From its initial low point the curve begins to rise very slowly in the thirteenth and fourteenth centuries, and then faster during the fifteenth and sixteenth centuries until it reaches its first peak in the seventeenth. Then it declines slightly in the eighteenth, and much more in the nineteenth century, although there is a minor rise at the end of the eighteenth and the beginning of the nineteenth. In the twentieth century it soars to a point unprecedented in all the twenty-five hundred years of Western society.

Our hypothesis well accounts for these three maxima of war. The period from the end of the twelfth to the seventeenth century saw the profound transformation of the Euro-

[9] See the data for these countries in my *Dynamics*.

pean system of values from the medieval ideational to the modern sensate. The ideational values were disintegrating and the modern sensate system was not matured.[10] The atomization and relativization of values resulted in the collapse of their stabilizing power. Their incompatibility — interindividual, intergroup, and interstate — became much greater than before. Hence, an increase of international as well as civil wars throughout Europe. But by the seventeenth century Europe had attained a new integrated system of ultimate values. Disintegration gave way to integration. Consequently there occurred the decline of the curve of war-magnitude during the eighteenth and the nineteenth century.

Its temporary rise at the end of the eighteenth and at the beginning of the nineteenth century is easily explained. It was due to the clash between those who wanted to liquidate the last remnants of the feudal order and the ideational culture and those who wanted to preserve them. After this short-lived clash, the curve of war markedly declined throughout the nineteenth century. These decades were the zenith of a well-integrated sensate culture and social order. The clash of values within the European universe was at its minimum. Hence the peaceful character of these decades.

With the beginning of the twentieth century we witness a rapid disintegration of sensate culture.[11] All its values were relativized and atomized to such an extent that none of them remained universally valid. Marriage, private property, God — all these values were undermined, criticized, and ground to dust. Social anarchy became supreme. No single value was recognized as binding equally the Hitlerites and anti-Hitlerites, Communists and capitalists, rich and poor, religious believers and atheists. As a result, the values lost a great deal of their restraining power. An ever increasing part of the population was guided by sensual, egotistic, and biological

[10] See the evidences in my *Dynamics*, in all four volumes.
[11] See the evidences in my *Dynamics*, all volumes, and in my *Crisis of Our Age* (New York, 1942).

impulses. Force and fraud became again the chief rulers of conduct.

This incompatibility of values, together with a tremendous growth of interindividual, intergroup, and intersocietal relationships, made inevitable an unprecedented explosion of civil and international wars. Thus we find ourselves in the bloodiest century of the last twenty-five hundred years of human history.

In this manner the actual maxima of war-magnitude in the history of at least ten countries (Greece, Rome, and eight European countries) unequivocally support our hypothesis.

I. Murder is individual war. What is the cause of murder, and how does it increase and decrease in the course of time? We know that murders are committed for many different reasons. In spite of this variety all murders have one and the same cause although their supplementary factors vary. The cause is the same as that of war. This is true of murders committed for material advantages, murders by fanaticists, murders of revenge, feud, passion, or insanity, and of murders for self-preservation. In all these cases, the cause is either the irreconcilable nature of the parties' basic values (murders of fanaticism, altruism, revenge, feud, passion), or an extreme atomization thereof (killings committed for material gain, self-preservation, or insanity). In the latter instance, these murderers are governed primarily by blind and disorganizing biological impulses. Both types reproduce in miniature the aforementioned condition of social *anomie*.

This theory of murder-causation is supported by the fact that persons with strongly integrated values do not commit murders of the second type, no matter how dire the emergency or how tempting the profit. My study shows that the percentage of persons taking the lives of their fellows during famine or other great emergencies is no more than one per cent. The rest may perish, but they will not slay.[12] Similarly,

[12] See my *Man and Society in Calamity* (New York, 1942), pp. 81-82 *et passim*.

murders of the first type (feud, revenge, passion, fanaticism) are committed only by persons whose norms are diametrically and uncompromisingly opposed to those of their victims.

J. Further evidence is offered by changes in the severity and extensity of punishment for crimes, especially capital punishment. Severe punishment is an index of irreconcilable conflict between those who punish and those who are punished. In this sense it is also a form of interindividual and group war. We know that the severity of punishment for crimes is not constant but fluctuates, in penal codes as well as in concrete practice, from period to period and from society to society. Elsewhere [13] the criminal codes of Greece, Rome, and of the main European countries have been studied in considerable detail. Changes in the severity of punishment both in the penal codes and in actual practice in these countries were systematically investigated. When the periods of increase and decrease of the severity of punishment were defined, the problem of the cause of these fluctuations was studied. The solution was as follows: *"Each time, when in a given group, the ethico-juridical heterogeneity and antagonism of its members increase, the amount as well as the severity of punishment imposed by one part of the society upon the other tends to increase; and, other conditions being equal, the greater the incompatibility, the greater is the increase."*[14] A sufficient body of evidence was given in *Dynamics* to demonstrate the validity of the proposition.

K. Finally, our proposition is supported by the inadequacy of all the other theories of the causes of war and peace. These take the form of either a theory of multiple causation or of some exclusive specific-factor hypothesis. The latter emphasizes some particular variable such as economic or political elements, sunspots, density and size of population, climate, etc. None of these, however, can stand even an elementary

[13] See my *Social and Cultural Dynamics*, Vol. II, pp. 515-627.
[14] *Ibid.*, p. 595. See there the factual corroboration.

test. One can take either mine or Professor Wright's war curves and try to explain their "ups and downs" in terms of any of these theories. The result is failure. These theories simply do not fit the data, and the data do not fit the theories.

The inadequacy of the multiple-causation type of theory has been set forth above. We may add one more point to that discussion. When multiple-causation assumes the form of some kind of equilibrium theory, stating that a change in any variable of the equilibrium system is one of the causes of war or peace, it does not get us anywhere. Since the variables are numerous, they are arbitrarily chosen from the countless antecedent conditions amidst which war or peace occurs. They remain incommensurable and incessantly varying in each case. The concept of equilibrium is inapplicable to social systems. This conclusion is reinforced strongly by Wright's attempt to use such a theory of multiple causation. In spite of the enormous material collected, and the many valuable contributions made, his attempt is unsuccessful. He leaves unsolved the problem of the causation of war and peace.[15]

Positive Evidence. Since I have presented most of the evidence under the heading "negative evidence," here I need mention only three of the more important corroborations.

A. The first concerns the minima of war in the history of Greece, Rome, and Europe. *In all these countries the minima of war or the maxima of peace fall exactly in the periods when the integration of their systems of values was high and the universe of the interacting states or nations was harmonious.*

In Greece before the fifth century B.C. the system of basic values was highly integrated. It was an ideational or religious-patriotic system permeating all compartments of Greek society and culture, unchallenged and unquestioned. It was essentially the same in practically all the Greek states. For this

---

[15] See Q. Wright, *A Study of War*, especially Volume II. See my criticism in *Ethics*, April, 1943. For a criticism of equilibrium theories see my *Dynamics*, Vol. IV, ch. 14.

reason we should expect a low level of war during this period. The facts show that such was the case. Wars did not disappear, of course, because the integration was not perfect, nor were incompatibilities in the secondary aspects of the system lacking, as in the communities of Sparta and Athens. From time to time the Greek states came into contact with quite different cultures, like the Persian, the values of which were far from compatible with their own. In these conditions wars broke out once in a while; but their magnitude was far below the level of the fifth and fourth centuries B.C.[16] After the fourth century B.C., the sensate system in Greece became dominant. The anarchy of the transition was over, and the values were reintegrated into a new sensate system. Hence the decline of the war-curves of Greece in the third and second centuries B.C.

In Rome the minima of war occurred in the fourth century B.C. and the first and second centuries A.D. These were the centuries of comparatively high integration of the Roman value-system. The great expansion of Rome did not begin until after the fourth century, and it was accomplished in all essentials by the beginning of our era.

A similar explanation holds for the comparatively low level of warfare in medieval Europe before the thirteenth century. During the Middle Ages the Christian system of values was highly integrated and universal for the whole of Europe. Sociocultural *anomie* was at its lowest ebb. Hence the small amount of warfare throughout these centuries. The relative recession of warfare in the eighteenth and nineteenth centuries followed the end of the transition from the ideational to a settled sensate system of values.

Thus, the minima of war have fallen in the periods in which they should have occurred according to our hypothesis. This conclusion is further reinforced by the corresponding data

[16] Detailed factual data on wars in Greece, Rome, and Europe can be found in my *Dynamics* and in Q. Wright's *A Study of War*.

for eight European nations studied separately. These include England, France, Russia, Austria, Italy, Spain, the Netherlands, and Poland-Lithuania.[17]

B. The minima of murder likewise fall in the periods of strong integration of the system of values. "Commercial murders" flourish uniformly in the societies where the value-system is in *anomic* state. Conversely there is a notable increase of murders in periods of transition, *anomie*, and great calamities.[18] The groups that permit such crimes are desocialized and demoralized, controlled mainly by disorganized biological impulses. On the other hand, in the periods of great and sudden increase in integration, murders notably decrease.[19]

C. A well established fact is the periodic mitigation and humanization of punishment imposed upon one part of the society by the other. Such relaxations of severity of punishment have regularly happened during epochs of social integration.[20]

The totality of the evidence given supports the proposed theory of the main cause of war sufficiently well, anyhow much better than any other hypothesis of the cause (s) of war. Insofar the theory deserves—even requires—a full attention of all those who directly or indirectly are busy with the business of war and especially with that of a lasting peace. As long as all these fool themselves (and others) by seemingly very concrete and very "practical" theories of the causes of peace they all are doomed to failure in their commendable plans to secure a lasting peace after this war. Just as these "practical" planners tragically failed, after the First World War, in their

[17] See the data in my *Dynamics*. The mortal defect of practically all the theories on war-causation is that their authors never troubled themselves to collect the complete data on the movement of wars and then verify their theories by these. They all have been just speculating and guessing.
[18] See the facts in my *Man and Society in Calamity*, chaps. x-xii.
[19] *Ibid.*
[20] See my *Dynamics*, Vol. II, chap xv.

endeavour to outlaw war, just as much they are going to fail
in the future as long as they take pseudo-causes of war and
peace for their real cause.

Next chapter briefly outlines the necessary conditions of a
lasting peace which directly follow from the above analysis
of the main cause and of the supplementary factors of war
(and peace).

CHAPTER ELEVEN

THE CONDITIONS AND POSSIBILITIES OF A LASTING PEACE IN THE POSTWAR PERIOD

1. *Main Reasons for the Failure of All Previous Plans and Efforts*

A lasting peace after this war is possible only if the cause of war is either eliminated or greatly diminished. Without this central step, no plans can succeed. Many suggested measures for the organization of a stable peace do not touch the real cause of war. For this reason they are doomed to failure. Indeed, many of these plans actually reinforce rather than remove the cause of war. They repeat the tragic errors of the Versailles Treaty. It is high time to stop this gambling with the lives of millions of human beings and to begin the organization of a lasting peace with the measures that really eliminate or limit the cause of war.

All the numerous plans and efforts for the establishment of a lasting peace have hitherto failed. The main reasons for such a failure have been two: first, objective sociocultural conditions have been unfavorable and unripe for such a venture; second, the measures proposed for the realization of a lasting peace have been inadequate.

A. *Unfavorable Objective Conditions.* These consisted, first of all, in the existence of a large number of societies with incompatible systems of values and in a lack of world-wide interaction and interdependence among the parts and groups of humanity. Mankind represented not one organism in which all nations, states, and large societies were interdependent, but a series of separate isolated nations, states, and societies without any common system of values and permanent ties binding them together. In such a situation a given society or nation could live and function without seriously affecting most of the other societies and without being affected by them. Clearly, in such a situation, without permanent interdependence, without social, economic, cultural or any other bonds linking mankind together, no international organization was possible. Lacking that, a universal and durable peace was likewise impossible. Each state or group or nation acted for itself and for its own interests without concern for the rest of humanity. Group egotisms or clash of the main values of these societies inevitably led to conflicts, which, in turn, inevitably led to war as the ultimate means for their solution. Under these circumstances any plan for a lasting *universal* peace was doomed to failure.

Another main obstacle to peace existing in objective socio-cultural reality has been the presence of a multitude of vested interests or conflicting values in each of these separate states, nations, and other groups. These interests or values have powerfully resisted the drastic reconstruction of the whole socio-cultural world which has become necessary for a successful establishment of lasting peace. As long as there existed a multitude of egotistic states or societies, each of these naturally opposed any limitation of their sovereignty, territorial independence, and advantage. Their governments and upper groups exerted all their power to keep their exalted position, with its privileges and advantages. Most of the religious, cultural, and other groups within these states acted in a similar manner as soon as any attempt was made to modify their conditions.

In brief, innumerable vested interests or conflicting values powerfully resisted — and had to resist — any plan, any effort toward the fundamental changes required for the establishment of a lasting peace. Planners of such a peace were in the position of the planner of an ideal city prohibited to tear down, to alter, or even to touch any existing building, from tenement house to mansion, any crooked street, any breeding place of disease or focus of infection. Clearly, no planner can build a healthful and beautiful city under these conditions. At best he can only repaint or slightly remodel a few of the buildings; but such a "renovation" does not create a new city. Under just such restrictions have labored all those who from time immemorial have dreamed of the building of a City of Eternal Peace. They were doomed to be mere Utopian dreamers and practical failures, thwarted by the gigantic resistance of the conflicting values of most of the existing social, political, economic, and cultural groups.

B. *Inadequacy of the Measures Proposed.* The second main reason for the failure of plans for peace consisted in the inadequacy of the measures proposed. Most of the planners have fooled themselves and others into believing that by a slight repainting and remodeling of the surface of a few social and political institutions — that is, by a mere superficial alteration of the existing political or economic conditions, supplemented by still more superficial "educational" and "cultural" measures — they can construct the greatest building of the world — the Temple of Eternal Peace. Such miracles do not happen in the construction of ordinary material buildings, let alone in the creation of the greatest social institutions. In both cases, the materials used and the methods employed must be adequate to the desired objective. Practically all plans for lasting peace, beginning with the ancient ones and ending with the most recent, have suffered from this inadequacy; namely, that the measures proposed for the achievement of a lasting peace have been utterly insufficient for the purpose. They consisted mainly in a new, but very modest, rearrangement of the number of sovereign states, of their boundaries, of their political systems, of international trade and commerce and the monetary system, of natural resources, and the like. It can be stated unequivocally that these measures cannot produce a lasting peace. At the best they can create only a temporary armistice; and even this is uncertain. These very measures were applied after the First World War. The results were appalling: instead of a lasting peace they created the most destructive, terrible, and gigantic war. Repetition of the same measures, even in a new variation, can yield not a lasting peace but new wars still more terrible than the present one. These plans are inadequate because they hardly mention four conditions without which no realization of a lasting peace is possible.

2. *Four Indispensable Conditions for a Lasting Peace*

These indispensable conditions are as follows: first, a fundamental reintegration and transvaluation of most of the contemporary cultural values; second, effective promulgation and inculcation among all states, nations, and social groups of a set of fundamental norms and values which shall be universally binding; third, explicit limitation of the sovereignty of all states in regard to war and peace; and fourth, the establishment of a supreme international authority vested with the power of obligatory and enforced decision in all international conflicts.

A. The first great step is the reintegration of the basic values so as to terminate the existing *anomie* and its consequences. To offset the current atomization and relativization, the process of universalizing the main values and their norms of conduct must be energetically pushed. Purely sensate values without the super-sensate, spiritual values cannot be universal. They can only be increasingly atomized. Hence a transvaluation of the present sensate norms by coalescence with more spiritual principles as end-values becomes inescapable. It is clear that a profound mental and moral revolution to make the dominant mentality more idealistic and spiritual is urgent. Those who do not like these terms can substitute more neutral ones such as the *categoric imperative, unconditional social duty,* and the like. When a given norm of conduct is regarded as obligatory and sacred, it becomes a transcendental value over and above utilitarian and hedonistic standards.[1]

B. We cannot make identical all the religious, ethical, and juridical norms, aesthetic values, or economic and political organizations of peoples and diverse cultures. But we can make them compatible by universalizing their basic norms of conduct. Without the organization of a moral universe no lasting peace is possible, no matter what economic or political reforms are made. No treaty or contract can bind if the parties concerned are cynical, nihilistic, free from the categorical imperative of prescribed norms and values. If not the sublimest norms of the Sermon on the Mount, which transcend the power of most mortals, then an approximation to these norms in the form of the imperatives: "Do not do to other groups what you would not like to have done to your group" and "Do to other groups what you would like to have done to your group" must be promulgated and deeply grafted into the heart and soul, into the mind and actual conduct of all human beings and of all states, nations, peoples, and their leaders, before a lasting peace can really be established.

The preceding chapter on the cause of war shows that the main or the necessary cause of war is an irreconcilability of the systems of norms and values which regulate either one or all of the belligerent societies. Without such a discrepancy — or conflict — of norms, no herd instinct, imperialism, nationalism, race difference, or any other economic or political cause can produce or ever has produced war. When such an atomization and conflict of the value systems of the two or more societies is given, the slightest event can produce and does produce the explosion. War has grown enormously precisely in periods of such disintegration and discrepancy. If such is

[1] For details see my *Crisis of Our Age.*

the necessary cause of war, obviously it must be removed or attacked before a lasting peace can be established. Without its removal all other measures are in vain.

These norms of the Golden Rule can be universally inculcated if all societies proclaim them as the basis of their constitution and interrelations; and if all their forces earnestly engage in implanting these norms into the actual behavior of their members, beginning with the preschool children and ending with the grownups, through the family, the school, the church, press, radio, and all the available means of education and formation of character and behavior. The inculcation must be so deep that the norms will become sacred, universal, and actually binding for all.

Leaving the details out of consideration in this paper, the essence of the proposition remains perfectly clear. All plans for lasting peace which disregard it or view it as a mere detail or pious wish are doomed to failure: they fool even their authors. For without this minimum of moral organization no lasting peace is possible. One can hardly expect a lasting peace among double-crossers and gangsters, no matter what treaties, contracts, and covenants they make. Likewise, without the realization of the above norms, all the high-sounding phrases about democracy and democratic peace are either empty or hypocritical, for any regime or social relationship that contradicts the terms of such a peace is not and cannot be truly democratic. So-called "democracies," devoid of this principle, are nothing but egotistic, corrupt, and predatory political machines, as bad as any coercive autocracy.

If the "practical" men object that the inculcation of such norms is impossible, and if for a moment we admit that they are right (while in fact they are wrong), this means only that a lasting and truly just or democratic peace is impossible, and therefore, any attempt to establish it is to be discounted once and for all. For without the realization of this condition mankind is doomed to have war as much as ever before in its previous history. If we want to decrease the catastrophe of war, the above norms governing relationships among individuals must be extended to all intergroup relationships, beginning with relationships between states and nations. There is no alternative possible.

C. The third indispensable condition for a lasting peace is an explicit limitation of the sovereignty of all states in all matters concerning war. The governments of all states must be explicitly deprived of the right to start war, just as such a right does not belong now either to chambers of commerce or to universities or to any social institution except the state and its government. As long as there are many states, each sovereign in these matters, with their more than fallible governments, there always will be wars. This is especially true of the contemporary state-leviathans with their mediocre, often cynical, frequently selfish, and invariably shortsighted governments. In spite of all the Holy Alliances, Triple Alliances, Quadruple Alliances, Balance of Power systems, Ententes, and Pan-Asiatic or Pan-American Unions, war did not disappear, often did not even decrease, as long as the sovereign states with their group-egotisms existed. In spite of the recent League of Nations, the Hague Court of Arbitration, numerous international conferences and pacts aimed at eliminating war, war was not abolished. On the contrary, the League of Nations and these pacts and conferences resulted in the most monstrous war in human history. With the state-leviathans left sovereign and with their governments left at liberty to decide war and peace, a repetition of these attempts cannot give lasting peace to tortured humanity. Such miracles do not happen, especially in the contemporary cynical and nihilistic world.

Again, if someone should say that such an explicit limitation of state-sovereignty is impossible, and if his statement were valid, this would mean only that a lasting peace is impossible, and that there is hence no need to fool ourselves and others with hopeless attempts. If we want such a peace, the sovereignty of all states in these matters must be abolished, and the abolition must be carried through in fact, with all the practical measures and consequences that follow from it.

D. The fourth indispensable condition of a lasting peace is the creation of a real, efficient, and powerful international authority empowered with the right of decision in all international conflicts between all states (and many other groups), and with power to enforce its verdicts. This international body must be alone sovereign in all matters concerning war and peace, with the proviso that its decisions are final (unless they are reconsidered by the body itself) and that in these decisions it is guided by the above norms, and that war as a rule would either be entirely eliminated or, would be used as a punitive measure against the violating group only in rare cases and on a small scale, with the elimination of all the most destructive and inhuman aspects of war.

It is beyond the concern of this short chapter to enter into the details of the technical organization and functions of such an international body. One remark is, however, necessary. Such an international body must consist not only of the representatives of the states, as in all previous alliances and unions and in the League of Nations, but also of the representatives of the world religions, science, fine arts, agriculture, and industrial labor and management. One of the main defects of all previous alliances and of the League of Nations was that they were made up only of the representatives of political groups. But the state is not the only important social organization. Side by side with it and no less important — indeed, from the point of view of creativeness, much more important — are other organizations: religious, scientific, artistic, economic, and familistic. They have contributed to the progress of mankind no less, but rather more, than the states. The states that hitherto monopolized the business of war are much more liable to be militant and to recur to war much more easily than these other great social organizations. Creative values of a great religion, of science, of fine arts, of industry and agriculture, of the family are much more peaceful and much less militant than the interests of the states and especially of their fallible governments. The role of the great non-political organizations has been highly constructive in the history of mankind and certainly less destructive than the role of the states. The influence and power of these organizations is again enormous. The presence of their representative leaders among the full-fledged members of the great international body would increase its wisdom and its knowledge, would ennoble it ethically and juridically, and would enormously reinforce its social, scientific, ethical and juridical prestige. In such a form it could become indeed the mouthpiece of human wisdom, the Supreme Court of Human Justice.

Almost all the existing plans for an international authority limit its composition to the representatives of the states. This decisive shortcoming must be eliminated and remedied by the inclusion of the representatives of other great social and cultural organizations like the ones mentioned above. Otherwise, the super-state leviathan of a new league of nations would exhibit all the vices of the old state egotism, and would repeat all the failings of the League of Nations. It may even turn into a veritable world-tyranny.

If again someone objects that such an international body cannot be created the answer is then in that case no lasting peace can be established.

Such are, in a rough black-and-white sketch, the four conditions that logically and inductively are necessary for the realization of a lasting peace.

3. Is the Proposed Plan Realizable?

In the past, for the reasons indicated above, the plan for a lasting peace, based upon the four conditions, outlined above, could not be realized at all. Even at the present time, were the world undergoing none of the recent wars, famines, epidemics, revolutions, and other calamities; if all mankind were not in one of the greatest crises in its history, the plan would be Utopian and could not be put through at all. But given the present catastrophe the situation has become entirely different. If we earnestly want a lasting peace, its realization is now within our reach. This is stated not as a pious wish, but as a practical proposal.

The reasons for the present opportunity are not far to seek. First, mankind is already bound together into one whole by hundreds of social, cultural, economic, technological, and political ties. Any important change in any important part of human society tangibly influences the rest. There is no possibility any more to build — for good or for evil — one society or nation without regard for all the others: all the other societies will be influenced by such a building and the building will be influenced, made possible or impossible, by the rest of the societies. Times of isolationism, in this broad sense, are irrevocably over. We live and act in a truly world-wide society. Regardless of our wishes, we cannot have a lasting peace for one country without having it for the rest of mankind. We cannot build a happy, wise, and prosperous society of our own while neglecting the rest of humanity. This means that the basis for a universal lasting peace is already created, and that lasting peace is possible only on a universal scale. No local lasting peace is any longer possible. Thus the first of the main obstacles to a lasting peace is already eliminated.

Likewise, the second main obstacle — the resistance of the vested interests or conflicting values of the existing states and other groups — is also greatly, indeed decisively, weakened. There is hardly any ground for the states to resist a limitation of their sovereignty, since the sovereignties of most of the states are already smashed and trampled upon, as witness the fact that for the last few decades states have appeared and disappeared like so many soap bubbles. There is no ground for the states to cling to their previous boundaries, because the latter are already effaced and in most cases their restoration is impossible. For the last few decades political boundaries have been changing incessantly, and have become perfectly fluid, insecure, and uncertain. Most of the governments existing before World War I do not exist any more; and most of the governments functioning before 1939 are now mere refugees; while most of those that exist now, including the dictatorships, will be replaced within the next few years, or at the longest, one or two decades. The political visions of the vested interests have been turned into short-lived dreams or faded memories, and, with continued anarchy, will continue to be, in ever-increasing tempo. Hopes to restore these ever-changing and mutually antagonistic governments are entirely hopeless. No great revolution restores any of its previous governments and previous aristocracies for a lasting time; they are dismissed once and for all. And the contemporary crisis is the greatest of all the revolutions of which we know.

Even the upper classes of the recent or present societies do not have any serious ground to oppose the great change. Their position also has become precarious and short-lived, lasting less than one generation. Since 1914 in most Western and some Eastern countries, two or three waves of different "aristocracies" have already replaced one another. Each new wave of these "khalifs for a day" is rapidly followed by a wave of newcomers, who in their turn disappear. None of these "aristocracies" can hope to be restored to its exalted *status quo ante*. In these conditions they neither have the power to oppose the great reform, nor have they even a vital interest in doing so.

The other well-to-do, professional, and middle classes are actually victims ruined or half-ruined by the existing condition of interstate war and anarchy. They can lose nothing by the great reconstruction except humiliation, hardship, and suffering.

To the rest of mankind, to the overwhelming majority of the rank and file, from peasant and laborer to merchant and clerk, from fathers and mothers to sons and daughters in all countries — to them the present wars of the sovereign states bring only utter misery, sorrow and death. These classes pay the largest bill of dead and wounded on the battlefields of the warring sovereign states, without glory or profit from their sacrifice. Since this misery and death are due to the continued anarchy of the multitudinous sovereign states, the bulk of humanity has no interest in preserving and perpetuating this anarchy, only in order to be subjected to an endless series of new catastrophes.

Finally, all decent persons with an elementary ethical sense and social responsibility cannot but hope for the elimination of the anarchical multitude of sovereign states, now the source of one of the greatest infections upon the human race.

Thus, with the exception of an insignificant number of human vultures, neither the states as states, nor their past and present governments, nor any of the important segments of humanity as a whole can profit from the present situation, can hold their interests intact, or can hope either to restore their *status quo ante* or to build a new and happy life within the old framework. Instead of this they all find themselves amidst the ruins of not only their personal well-being and happiness but of the whole previous social, cultural, political, and economic edifice. A restoration of these ruins to the *status quo ante* is impossible; if modified slightly, the restoration promises only a repetition of old catastrophies. The sovereign states that had rendered a great service in the past now have become a source of perdition.

If a city is demolished by calamity, wise planners of a new city do not simply restore the demolished one, with all its defects and shortcomings. They try to build a new city free from the defects of the old and incorporating in itself the maximum of utility, health, and beauty. In such a reconstruction all the ancient vested interests are shoved aside, from the owners of ruined tenements and houses of vice to the millionaire dealers in crime, corruption, and public waste.

Our generation and the next are placed amid the ruins of the sociocultural world. We must plan to build a new society as free from war as is humanly possible. Since the vested interests of the past are already shattered, they cannot oppose our plans successfully. History gives us the unique opportunity of a wide freedom from the pressures of reactionary opposition. If humanity and its true leaders determine to build the great new society largely free from war, they can do it. What in the past was unattainable and Utopian, now, under present conditions, becomes realizable. With vision, courage, and faith, we can, to the greater glory of God and the greater nobility of man, build the Temple of Lasting Peace.

INDEX

INDEX